2002-2003
Edition

Ten-Tronck's™

Celebrity Web Site
&
E-Mail Directory

Published by:

 Axiom Information Resources

Ann Arbor, Michigan 48107

Celebrity Web Site & E-Mail Directory™
Published by Axiom Information Resources, Inc.
Ann Arbor, Michigan 48107 USA

Published by:
Axiom Information Resources, Inc.
P.O. Box 8015
Ann Arbor, MI 48107

Printed in USA
ISBN 0-943213-45-2
ISSN 1524-8704

Cover Design by: Concialdi Design

SPECIAL SALES
The Celebrity Web Site & E-Mail Directory™ is
available at special quantity discounts
for bulk purchases. For information write:

Axiom Information Resources, Inc.
P.O. Box 8015-WEB#21
Ann Arbor, MI 48107

Contents

Order Blank and Customer Response Form (See Back Page)

Introduction

Welcome to the *Celebrity Web Site & E-Mail Directory*. This book will serve as an easy-to-use, one-stop guide to the coolest Web Sites and E-Mail addresses of Movie and TV stars, recording artists, athletes, politicians, and assorted other celebrities.

Researchers, librarians, and fans alike will find this to be an invaluable resource. Web sites provide a wealth of information about your favorite celebrities. If you want filmographies, appearance schedules, or biographical facts about a movie star, their web sites are a good place to look. If you want the latest touring schedule or recording information about your favorite singer or music group, it's probably posted on their web site. Or if you want to chat with other fans or purchase merchandise such as T-shirts or CD's, their web site is your best bet.

This book will also help you to send E-mail messages to celebrities. Although some celebrities do not make their E-mail addresses public, they will often provide alternate ways to contact them at their web sites, so it's always a good idea to check there if you're looking to contact celebrities for whatever reason.

A final note: if you find a celebrity's official web-site or E-mail address that is not listed in this book, please let us know by contacting us at http:www.celebritylocator.com.

The Celebrity Web Site & E-Mail Directory's Top Five celebrity Web sites:

1. Michael Jackson: http://www.mjifc.com/

2. Prince Charles: http://www.princeofwales.gov.uk/

3. Tiger Woods: http://www.tigerwoods.com/

4. Madonna: http://www.madonnanet.com/guide/

5. Leonard Nimoy: http://www.nimoy.com/

Movies/TV

A _____ A

Abbott And Costello
http://www.abbottandcostello.net/

Ben Affleck
http://benaffleck.com/

John Agar
http://www.johnagar.com/

Jenny Agutter
http://www.tmaw.webfusion.co.uk/jennya.html

Kristian Alfonso
http://www.geocities.com/TelevisionCity/Stage/4941/enter.html

Tatyana Ali
http://www.tatyanaali.com/

Chad Allen
http://www.geocities.com/WestHollywood/Heights/8274/

Jonelle Allen
http://www-personal.umich.edu/~jcoles/jaindex.html

Karen Allen
http://www.acmewebpages.com/karen_a/index.html

Tim Allen
http://www.geocities.com/Hollywood/Set/1067/timpage.htm

Woody Allen
http://www.woodyallen.com/

Carol Alt
http://www.carolalt.net/

A Martinez
http://www.amartinez.com/

If you find some dead links, please let us know at: http://www.celebritylocator.com/

Gillian Anderson
http://gaws.ao.net/

Richard Dean Anderson
http://rdanderson.com/

Pamela Anderson-Lee
http://www.pamelaandersonlee.com/

Real Andrews
http://www.realandrews.net/

Vanessa Angel
http://www.mca.com/tv/weirdscience/cast/angel.html

Jennifer Aniston
http://www.perfectpixs.com/aniston/links.htm

Ann-Margret
http://www.ann-margret.com/

Gabrielle Anwar
http://www.candy-fans.com/anwar/index.html

Christina Applegate
http://www.christina-applegate.com/

Adam Arkin
http://www.geocities.com/Hollywood/5093/

Beatrice Arthur
http://www.mbcnet.org/ETV/A/htmlA/arthurbeatr/arthurbeatr.htm

Jane Asher
http://www.jane-asher.co.uk/

Rowan Atkinson
http://www.dsv.su.se/~mats-bjo/bean/bean.html

Dan Aykroyd
http://www.geocities.com/Tokyo/3948/aykroyd.html

If you find some dead links, please let us know at: http://www.celebritylocator.com/

B
B

Dr. Mohan Babu
http://www.mohanbabu.com/

Laureen Bacall
http://themave.com/Bacall/

Kevin Bacon
http://www.geocities.com/~ohmystars/

Shaune Bagwell
http://www.shaunebagwell.com/

Scott Bairstow
http://www.henge.com/~swanson/

Alec Baldwin
http://www.konary.com/alec/alec.html

Daniel Baldwin
http://www.danielbaldwin.net/

Christian Bale
http://www.christianbale.org/

Antonio Banderas
http://www.antoniobanderasfans.com/abmain.htm

Adrienne Barbeau
http://www.abarbeau.com/

Julia Rose Barr
http://www.juliarosebarr.com/

Majel Barrett-Roddenberry
http://www.roddenberry.com/

Sara Barrett
http://www.sarabarrett.com/

Drew Barrymore
http://www.drew-barrymore.com/

If you find some dead links, please let us know at: http://www.celebritylocator.com/

Blake Bashoff
http://www.blakebashoff.com/

Angela Bassett
http://members.tripod.com/~bholness/angela.html

Patrick Bauchau
http://www.bauchau.com/

Jaime Bauer
http://www.jaimelynbauer.com/

Michelle Bauer
http://www.picpal.com/picpal/mbauer.html

Meredith Baxter
http://www.meredithbaxter.org/

Mr. Bean
http://www.mrbean.co.uk/

Emmanuelle Beart
http://sunflower.singnet.com.sg/~swying/emmanuelle.html

Shari Belafonte
http://www.sharibelafonte.com/

Cathrine Bell
http://www.ocbfc.com/

Robert Beltran
http://www.robertbeltran.com/

Michael Bergin
http://www.geocities.com/WestHollywood/Parade/5765/

Ingrid Bergman
http://www.cmgww.com/stars/bergman/

Halle Berry
http://www.geocities.com/Hollywood/Set/1592/Halle.html

Michael Biehn
http://www.tropicalshade.com/michael/

If you find some dead links, please let us know at: http://www.celebritylocator.com/

Juliette Binoche
http://www.binoche.com/

Thora Birch
http://www.thora.org/

Bill Blair
http://www.alienactor.com/

Linda Blair
http://www.lindablair.com/

Fairuza Blak
http://www.fairuza.com/

Yasmine Bleeth
http://www.yasmine-bleeth.org/

Humphrey Bogart
http://www.macconsult.com/bogart/

Ron Bohmer
http://www.ronbohmer.com/

Lisa Bonet
http://www.groupiecentral.com/gwllisab.html

Evan Bonifant
http://www.geocities.com/ebmainpage/

Felicity Brewis-Pawellek
http://felicity.connect.to/

Jeff Bridges
http://www.jeffbridges.com/

Sarah Brightman
http://www.sarahbrightman.co.uk/

Charles Bronson
http://www.geocities.com/Hollywood/Set/5040/

Avery Brooks
http://www.geocities.com/Hollywood/8914/

If you find some dead links, please let us know at: http://www.celebritylocator.com/

Pierce Brosnan
http://www.mcs.net/~klast/www/brosnan.html

Clancy Brown
http://www.clancy-brown.com/

Jensen Buchanan
http://www.geocities.com/Hollywood/Bungalow/1482/

Betty Buckley
http://www.bettybuckley.com/

Sandra Bullock
http://sandra.com/

Delta Burke
http://www.deltaburke.com/

Brooke Burns
http://www.baywatchtv.com/cast/burns.html

Steve Burton
http://www.steveburton.net/

Sarah Buxton
http://www.sarahbuxton.com/

C _____ C

Ashley Lyn Cafagna
http://www.ashleycafagna.com/

Nicolas Cage
http://www.best.com/~toni/index.htm

Dean Cain
http://fantasia.simplenet.com/lnc/

Bruce Campbell
http://www.bruce-campbell.com/

Christian Campbell
http://www.official.christiancampbell.org/

If you find some dead links, please let us know at: http://www.celebritylocator.com/

Neve Campbell
http://www.nevecampbell.dk/

Drew Carey
http://virtuallot.warnerbros.com/cmp/comedy/cm01.htm

George Carlin
http://www.georgecarlin.com/

David Carradine
http://www.davidcarradine.org/

Jim Carrey
http://www.geocities.com/Hollywood/9090/

Angela Cartwright
http://www.angela-cartwright.com/

Veronica Cartwright
http://www.veronica-cartwright.com/

Jackie Chan
http://www.trade.net.hk/clients/jackiechan/

David Chokachi
http://davidchokachi.homestead.com/

Claudia Christian
http://www.claudiachristian.net/

Terry Ike Clanton
http://www.clantongang.com/oldwest/teryresu.html

Andrew Dice Clay
http://www.angelfire.com/ny2/diceman/

Kristen Cloke
http://www.kristencloke.com/

George Clooney
http://www.clooneyfiles.com/

Willie Colon
http://www.williecolon.com/

If you find some dead links, please let us know at: http://www.celebritylocator.com/

Holly Marie Combs
http://www.hollymariecombs.com/

Jennifer Connelly
http://www.jennifer-connelly.com/

Sean Connery
http://www.mcs.net/~klast/www/connery.html

Kevin Costner
http://www.geocities.com/Hollywood/7555/

Courteney Cox
http://www.courteneycox.net/

Peter Coyote
http://www.petercoyote.com/

Yvonne Craig
http://yvonnecraig.com/

Russell Crowe
http://www.csh.rit.edu/~halle/russell.html

MaCaulay Culkin
http://www.macaulayculkin.net/

Brett Cullen
http://www.brettcullen.com/

D _____ **D**

Timothy Dalton
http://www.timothydalton.com/

Matt Damon
http://mattdamon.com/

Claire Danes
http://www.clairedanes.com/

Rodney Dangerfield
http://www.rodney.com/

If you find some dead links, please let us know at: http://www.celebritylocator.com/

Linda Dano
http://www.lindadano.com/

Patrika Darbo
http://www.patrika-darbo.com/

Bette Davis
http://www.cmgww.com/stars/davis/

Daniel Day-Lewis
http://www.danielday.org/

Derek de Lint
http://www.execpc.com/~pewter/Derek_de_Lint/index.html

James Dean
http://www.jamesdean.com/

Calvert Deforest
http://www.calvertdeforest.com/

Dana Delany
http://www.danadelany.com/

Michael DeLorenzo
http://www.michaeldelorenzo.com/

Benicio Del Toro
http://www.beniciodeltoro.com/

Catherine Deneuve
http://www.generation.net/~vincy/cdeneuve.htm

Bob Denver
http://bobdenver.com/

Bo Derek
http://www.boderek.com/

Cameron Diaz
http://www.cameron-diaz.com/

Leonardo DiCaprio
http://www.leonardodicaprio.com/

If you find some dead links, please let us know at: http://www.celebritylocator.com/

Marlene Dietrich
http://www.marlene.com/

Andrew Divoff
http://www.andrewdivoff.com/

Shannen Doherty
http://www.shannen-doherty.simplenet.com

Ami Dolenz
http://www.amidolenz.com/

Lisa Donovan
http://www.lisadonovan.com/

Robert Downey Jr.
http://www.bserv.com/users/lesliv.htm

David Duchovny
http://www.duchovny.net/

Denice Duff
http://www.deniceduff.com/

E   E

Clint Eastwood
http://www.clinteastwood.net/

Shari Eckert
http://www.sharieckert.com/

Maggie Egan
http://www.maggieegan.com/

Nicole Eggert
http://www.geocities.com/Hollywood/2613/nicole.html

Carmen Electra
http://www.serve.com/carmen/

Jenna Elfman
http://www.microtec.net/~dhouston/

If you find some dead links, please let us know at: http://www.celebritylocator.com/

Shannon Elizabeth
http://www.shannonelizabeth.com/

Alison Elliott
http://members.aol.com/Kidkinney/alison.html

Elvira
http://www.elvira.com/

Emilio Estevez
http://www.pacifier.com/~amye/

Andrea Evans
http://www.andreaevans.org/

Rupert Everett
http://www.geocities.com/Athens/Delphi/7724/index.html

F _____ **F**

Jeff Fahey
http://www.eskimo.com/~whtrose/fahey.html

Terry Farrell
http://www.TerryFarrell.net/

Ralph Fiennes
http://members.tripod.com/~ncampos/fienneses/index.html

Carrie Fisher
http://www.carriefisher.com/

Erroll Flynn
http://www.cmgww.com/stars/flynn/

Vivica Fox
http://www.vivicafox.com/

Jason David Frank
http://www.geocities.com/Hollywood/9324/jason.html

Jonathan Frid
http://www.jonathanfrid.com/

If you find some dead links, please let us know at: http://www.celebritylocator.com/

Annette Funicello
http://www.cowtown.net/users/annette/

Mira Furlan
http://www.mirafurlan.com/

G   G

Clark Gable
http://www.gable.org/

David Gallagher
http://www.dgnews.net/

Judy Garland
http://www.zianet.com/jjohnson/contents.htm

Jennie Garth
http://www.jenniegarth.com/

Jennifer Gatti
http://www.jennifergatti.com/

Sarah Michelle Gellar
http://www.sarah-michelle-gellar.com/

Gina Gershon
http://www.geocities.com/Paris/LeftBank/7614/gershon/

Deborah Gibson
http://www.deborah-gibson.com/

Mel Gibson
http://www.tropicalshade.com/melgibson/

Lillian Gish
http://www.cmgww.com/stars/gish/

Leigh-Davis Glass
http://www.leigh-davisglass.com/

Melanie Good
http://www.melaniegood.com/

If you find some dead links, please let us know at: http://www.celebritylocator.com/

Cary Grant
http://www.carygrant.net/

Hugh Grant
http://users.aol.com/gaelmcgear/hughtimeline.html

Red Green
http://www.redgreen.com/

Bruce Greenwood
http://brucegreenwood.com

Richard Grieco
http://www.rgrieco.com/

Melanie Grifth
http://www.melaniegriffith.com/

Jasmine Guy
http://www.jasmineguystar.com/

H _____ **H**

Larry Hagman
http://www.larryhagman.com/

Anthony Michael Hall
http://www.hallofmirrors.com/

Deidre Hall
http://www.marlena.com/

Jean Harlow
http://www.jeanharlow.com/

Linda Harrison
http://www.lindaharrison.com/

Susan Haskell
http://www.susanhaskell.com/

David Hasselhoff
http://www.davidhasselhoff.com/

If you find some dead links, please let us know at: http://www.celebritylocator.com/

Teri Hatcher
http://www.teri.net/

Shawn Hatosy
http://www.shawnhatosy.com/

Dennis Hayden
http://www.dennishayden.com/

Salma Hayek
http://www.geocities.com/Hollywood/Studio/1268/

Helen Hayes
http://www.cmgww.com/stars/hayes/

David Hedison
http://www.davidhedison.com/

Florence Henderson
http://www.flohome.com/

Audrey Hepburn
http://www.audreyhepburn.com/

Pee-Wee Herman
http://www.angelfire.com/mo/coolcat/

David Hess
http://www.davidhess.com/

Jennifer Love Hewittß
http://www.jennifer-love.com/

Cathrine Hickland
http://www.hickland.com/

Benny Hill
http://www.bennyhill.com/

Dustin Hoffman
http://www.sky.net/~emily/dustin.html

Bob Hope
http://www.bobhope.com/

If you find some dead links, please let us know at: http://www.celebritylocator.com/

Sir Anthony Hopkins
http://www.nasser.net/hopkins/

Lisa Howard
http://www.lisahoward.net/

Carol Hoyt
http://brent.simplenet.com/hoyt/

Tom Hulce
http://www.tomhulce.net/

Sammo Hung
http://www.sammohung.com/

Helen Hunt
http://stud2.tuwien.ac.at/~e9525634/

Elizebeth Hurley
http://www.geocities.com/Hollywood/Bungalow/1541/

William Hurt
http://www.eonline.com/Facts/People/0,12,47,00.html

Alex Hyde-White
http://www.alexhydewhite.com/

I _____ **I**

Boman Irani
http://www.bomanirani.com/

Michael Ironside
http://www.geocities.com/Hollywood/Hills/3227/

J _____ **J**

Joshua Jackson
http://www.angelfire.com/mt/pacey/

Samuel L. Jackson
http://member.aol.com/gifhack/main.html

If you find some dead links, please let us know at: http://www.celebritylocator.com/

Ann Jillian
http://www.annjillian.com/

Amy Jo Johnson
http://www.amyjojohnson.com/

Don Johnson
http://www.donjohnson.com/

James Earl Jones
http://www.geocities.com/Hollywood/1585/index.html

Shirley Jones
http://www.shirleyjones.com/

Tommy Lee Jones
http://members.aol.com/lukoch2/index.htm

Milla Jovovich
http://www.millaj.com/

K _____ K

Stacy Kamano
http://www.stacykamano.com/

Mitzi Kapture
http://members.xoom.com/intrinsic/mitzi.htm

Peter Karrie
http://www.peterkarrie.com/

Andy Kaufman
http://andykaufman.jvlnet.com/

Buster Keaton
http://www.busterkeaton.com/

DeForester Kelley
http://www.DeForestKelley.org/

Princess Grace Kelly
http://members.tripod.com/~gracepage/

If you find some dead links, please let us know at: http://www.celebritylocator.com/

Jamie Kennedy
http://www.jamiekennedy.com/

Nicole Kidman
http://www.nicolekidman.org/

Val Kilmer
http://www.geocities.com/Hollywood/4532/z11indx.htm

Roslyn Kind
http://www.roslynkind.com/

Sally Kirkland
http://www.sallykirkland.com/

Kevin Kline
http://members.nbci.com/dramafan/kevinkline/index.html

Bernie Kopell
http://www.berniekopell.com/

Lisa Kudrow
http://www.geocities.com/Hollywood/3142/kudrow.htm

L   L

Alan Ladd
http://www.cmgww.com/stars/ladd/

Cheryl Ladd
http://www.cherylladd.com/

David Lago
http://www.davidlago.com/

Ricki Lake
http://www.ricki.com/

Dorothy Lamour
http://www.cmgww.com/stars/lamour/

Nathan Lane
http://www.nathanlane.com/

If you find some dead links, please let us know at: http://www.celebritylocator.com/

A.J. Langer
http://www.geocities.com/TelevisionCity/Studio/1042/

Anthony Lapaglia
http://www.geocities.com/TheTropics/8175/lapaglia.htm

Laurel and Hardy
http://www.laurel-and-hardy.com/

Jamie Lauren
http://www.jamielauren.com/

Lucy Lawless
http://www.xenafan.com/

Christopher Lawrence
http://www.geocities.com/Hollywood/Lot/3668/

Martin Lawrence
http://www.martin-lawrence.com/

Sharon Lawrence
http://sharon-lawrence.com/

George Lazenby
http://www.mcs.net/~klast/www/lazenby.html

Kelly LeBrock
http://www.kellylebrock.net/

Brandy Ledford
http://www.brandyledford.com/

Bruce Lee
http://www.teleport.com/~danlucas/bruce.html

Jason Scott Lee
http://www.jasonscottlee.com/

Hudson Leick
http://www.hudsonleickfan.com/

Jay Leno
http://www.nbc.com/tonightshow/

If you find some dead links, please let us know at: http://www.celebritylocator.com/

Laura Linney
http://www.geocities.com/Hollywood/1404/

Barry Livingston
http://www.mythreesons-ernie.com/

Eric Lloyd
http://www.ericlloyd.com/

Ann Lockhart
http://www.annelockhart.com/

Heather Locklear
http://www.jimsplace.com/jim/hl.htm

Corina Logan
http://www.corinalogan.com/

Jennifer Lopez
http://www.jenniferlopez.com/

Mario Lopez
http://www.mario-lopez.com/

Sophia Loren
http://www.sophialoren.com/

BarBara Luna
http://members.aol.com/lunaact/

Dawn Lyn
http://www.tvtoys.com/my3sons/

M _____ M

Andie MacDowell
http://web.pinknet.cz/AndieMacDowell/

Kyle MacLachlan
http://www.geocities.com/Hollywood/5286/Kyle/kyle.html

If you find some dead links, please let us know at: http://www.celebritylocator.com/

Michael Madsen
http://www.michaelmadsen.com./
(another Michael Madsen site)
http://members.aol.com/madsen1fan/pp22.htm

Andrea Marcovicci
http://www.marcovicci.com/

Cindy Margolis
http://www.cindymargolis.com/

Julianna Margulies
http://www.fotomayer.de/jules/new/default.htm

Kellie Maroney
http://www.kellimaroney.com/

Jason Marsden
http://www.phoenix.net/~elissa/jason.htm

James Marshall
http://www.ismi.net/~joemill/

James Marsters
http://www.james-marsters.com/

Dean Martin
http://www.deanmartinfancenter.com/

Kellie Martin
http://www.joes.com/home/markrabo/

Steve Martin
http://www.stevemartin.com/

A Martinez
http://www.amartinez.com/

Chase Masterson
http://www.chasemasterson.com/

Cameron Mathison
http://www.cameronmathison.com/

If you find some dead links, please let us know at: http://www.celebritylocator.com/

Joseph Mazzello
http://www.he.net/~mike/

Jenny McCarthy
http://www.jenny-mccarthy.com/

Matthew McConaughey
http://www.flash.net/~rana2kay/MattMcPage.html

Eric McCormack
http://www.ericmccormack.com/

Lisa Raye McCoy
http://www.lisaraye.com/

Dyland McDermott
http://www.capecod.net/~ehahn/dmcdermott/dylan.html

Ryan Christopher McFadden
http://www.ryanchristopher.com/

William McNamara
http://www.williammcnamara.com/

Tamara Mello
http://www.tamara-mello.com/

Rena Mero
http://www.renamero.com/

Mark Metcalf
http://www.geocities.com/Hollywood/Hills/8018/

Jonathan Rhys Meyers
http://www.jrm-uk.co.uk/

Dale Midkiff
http://www.geocities.com/TelevisionCity/Studio/1383/

Alyssa Milano
http://www.alyssa.com/

Hayley Mills
http://www.geocities.com/Yosemite/2505/

If you find some dead links, please let us know at: http://www.celebritylocator.com/

Helen Mirren
http://www.helenmirren.com/

Alfred Molina
http://www.alfred-molina.com/

Marilyn Monroe
http://www.marilynmonroe.com/

Elizabeth Montgomery
http://members.aol.com/LizMontFan/LizMontPage.html

Demi Moore
http://www.demimoore.org/

Julianne Moore
http://www.julianne-moore.com/

Roger Moore
http://www.roger-moore.com/
(Another Roger Moore Site)
http://www.mcs.net/~klast/www/moore.html

Shemar Moore
http://www.shemar.com/

James Morrison
http://www.mindspring.com/~louisep/jmdg-l/

Bill Mumy
http://www.billmumy.com/

The Munster (TV Show)
http://www.munsters.com/

Ellen Muth
http://www.ellenmuth.net/

N _____ **N**

Liam Neeson
http://www.geocities.com/Hollywood/Set/6510/

If you find some dead links, please let us know at: http://www.celebritylocator.com/

Sam Neill
http://www.samneill.com/

Nichelle Nichols
http://www.uhura.com/

Jack Nicholson
http://www.triviatribute.com/jacknicholson.html

Leonard Nimoy
http://www.nimoy.com/

Barbara Niven
http://www.barbaraniven.com/

David Niven
http://www.cmgww.com/stars/niven/

Gena Lee Nolin
http://www.genalee.com/

Kathleen Noone
http://www.allmediapr.com/noone/

Chris North
http://members.aol.com/dwalheim/noth.html

Bill Nye
http://www.nyelabs.com

O _____ O

Renee O'Connor
http://rampages.onramp.net/~rocweb/

Chris O'Donnell
http://rs2.ch.liv.ac.uk/biry/chris_odonnell.html

Rosie O'Donnell
http://rosieo.warnerbros.com/

David O'Hara
http://www.wardy.org/ohara.html

If you find some dead links, please let us know at: http://www.celebritylocator.com/

Maureen O'Hara
http://maureenohara.com/

Gary Oldman
http://home.worldonline.nl/~giso/oldman.htm

Larisa Oleynik
http://www.larisaoleynik.com/

Alberto Olmedo
http://www.olmedo.com.ar/

Edward James Olmos
http://xwing.t-one.net/olmos/

Julia Ormond
http://www.vancouver.net/home/cacchioni/julia.htm

P _____ P

Al Pacino
http://www.alpacino.com/

Kelly Packard
http://www.baywatchtv.com/cast/packard.html

Elaine Paige
http://www.elainepaige.com/

Gwyneth Paltrow
http://www.gwynethpaltrow.org/

Vanessa Paradis
http://www.vanessaparadis.net/

Michael Pare
http://www.MichaelPare.com/

Sarah Jessica Parker
http://www.geocities.com/Hollywood/5159/

Trey Parker
http://www.geocities.com/TelevisionCity/Studio/1751/trey.html

If you find some dead links, please let us know at: http://www.celebritylocator.com/

Butch Patrick
http://www.munsters.com/

Adrian Paul
http://www.unl.edu/uevents/mine/adrian.html

Austin Peck
http://www.austinpeck.com/

Bettie Page
http://www.cmgww.com/stars/page/

Melody Patterson
http://www.melodypatterson.com/

Nia Peeples
http://www.niapeeples.net/

Ashley Peldon
http://www.courtneypeldon.com/

Courtney Peldon
http://www.courtneypeldon.com/

Sean Penn
http://www.geocities.com/Hollywood/Bungalow/6339/

Vincent Perez
http://www.vincentperez.com/

Luke Perry
http://www.flash.net/~narnia/luke.htm

Matthew Perry
http://www.matthewperry.org/

Joe Pesci
http://pesci.tierranet.com/joepesci/

Bernadette Peters
http://www.bernadettepeters.net/

Michelle Pfeiffer
http://www.michellepfeiffer.org/

If you find some dead links, please let us know at: http://www.celebritylocator.com/

Bratt Pitt
http://www.thezone.pair.com/celeb/pitt.htm

Carlos Ponce
http://www.carlosponce.com/

Natalie Portman
http://www.natalieportman.com/

Chris Potter
http://www.caine.com/cp/

Stephanie Powers
http://www.stefaniepowers.com

Freddie Prinze, Jr.
http://www.freddieprinzejr.com/

Q _____ Q

Aidan Quinn
http://www.mindspring.com/~angstgirl/aidan.html

R _____ R

Ingo Rademacher
http://www.ingo.net/

Lexi Randall
http://www.geocities.com/Hollywood/Boulevard/2538/

Lynn Redgrave
http://www.redgrave.com/

Keanu Reeves
http://www.keanunet.com/

Duncan Regehr
http://www.duncanregehr.com/

Brad Renfro
http://www.Bradrenfro.org/

If you find some dead links, please let us know at: http://www.celebritylocator.com/

Ernie Reyes, Jr.
http://www.erniereyesjr.com/

Burt Reynolds
http://www.burtreynolds.com/

Debbie Reynolds
http://www.debbiereynolds.com/

Tim Rice
http://home.earthlink.net/~jsjb/tim/tr.html

Ariana Richards
http://www.ariana.org/

Denise Richards
http://www.denisecentral.com/

Don Rickles
http://www.thehockeypuck.com/

Eric Roberts
http://www.ericrobertsactor.com/

Julia Roberts
http://web.pinknet.cz/~matusek/j_roberts/

Chris Rock
http://members.tripod.com/~Reco_Williams/CHRIS_ROCK.html

Roy Rogers
http://www.royrogers.com/

Will Rogers
http://www.ellensplace.net/rogers.html

Al Roker
http://www.roker.com/

Charlotte Ross
http://www.charlotteross.com/

If you find some dead links, please let us know at: http://www.celebritylocator.com/

Tim Roth
http://www.geocities.com/Hollywood/Lot/3753/TimIndex.html

Cynthia Rothrock
http://www.interlog.com/~tigger/rothrock.html

Keri Russell
http://www.kerirussell.net/

Kurt Russell
http://www.geocities.com/Paris/Bistro/7019/index.html

Kelly Rutherford
http://www.geocities.com/Hollywood/Hills/6813/kelly/index.html

Jeri Lynn Ryan
http://www.jerilynn.com/

Meg Ryan
http://web.pinknet.cz/~matusek/meg/

S _____ **S**

Antonio Sabato
http://www.geocities.com/Paris/LeftBank/3279/ANTONIO.HTML

Adam Sandler
http://www.adamsandler.com/
(another Adam Sandler site)
http://www.asandler.com/

Susan Sarandon
http://www.chrisbaker.co.uk/

Joe Scheibelhut
http://members.tripod.com/~planetjoe/

Rob Schneider
http://www.geocities.com/Hollywood/Set/6338/who.html

Tracy Scoggins
http://www.tracyscoggins.net/

If you find some dead links, please let us know at: http://www.celebritylocator.com/

Arnold Schwarzenegger
http://www.schwarzenegger.com/

David Schwimmer
http://users.aol.com/loraj/dspage.html

Jerry Seinfeld
http://www2.gvsu.edu/%7Emaurerb/Seinfeld.html

Jane Seymour
http://www.janeseymour.org/

Caryn Shalita
http://www.caryn.com/

William Shatner
http://www.williamshatner.com/

Helen Shaver
http://www.helen-shaver.com/

Cybill Shepherd
http://www.cybill.com/

Rhonda Shear
http://www.rhondashear.com/

Brooke Shields
http://www.geocities.com/Hollywood/Hills/2939/

Elisabeth Shue
http://www.elisabeth-shue.com/

Karen Sillas
http://www.karensillas.com/

Ron Silver
http://members.tripod.com/~Barbara_Robertson/silver.html

Alicia Silverstone
http://www.silverstone.org/

Richards Simmons
http://www.richardsimmons.com/

If you find some dead links, please let us know at: http://www.celebritylocator.com/

Gary Sinise
http://sinisefans.org/

Anna Nicole Smith
http://www.annaonline.com/

Taran Smith
http://members.aol.com/cammy1234/cktns.html

Smothers Brothers
http://www.smothersbrothers.com/

Kevin Sorbo
http://msmoo.simplenet.com/sorbo/sorbo4.htm

Louise Sorel
http://www.louisesorelinc.com/

Talisa Soto
http://members.tripod.com/~pandus/TALISASOTO.html

Kevin Spacey
http://www.spacey.com/

Brent Spiner
http://www.asahi-net.or.jp/~ti3y-itu/

Jessica Steen
http://www.jessicasteen.com/

Stella Stevens
http://www.stellastevens.com/

Patrick Stewart
http://www.patrickstewart.org/

Julia Stiles
http://www.julia-stiles.net/

Sharon Stone
http://www.serve.com/sharon/sharon.htm

Rider Strong
http://www.riderstrong.com/

If you find some dead links, please let us know at: http://www.celebritylocator.com/

Gloria Swanson
http://www.cmgww.com/stars/swanson/

Alison Sweeney
http://www.alisonsweeney.com/

T _____ **T**

Cary-Hiroyuki Tagawa
http://www.carytagawa.com/

Patricia Tallman
http://www.patriciatallman.com/

Elizabeth Taylor
http://users.deltanet.com/users/dstickne/lizt.htm

Sandi Taylor
http://www.sandi-taylor.com/

Tiffani-Amber Theissen
http://www.tiffaniambertheissen.com/

Charlize Theron
http://www.charlizetheron.com/

Damien Thomas
http://pages.citenet.net/users/ctmx3590/

Kristin Scott Thomas
http://djuna.simplenet.com/kst/

Tim Thomerson
http://hometown.aol.com/timthomfc/index.htm

Emma Thompson
http://www.muldermedia.com/emma/index.html

Courtney Thorne-Smith
http://www.courtneythornesmith.com/

The Three Stooges
http://www.3-stooges.com/

If you find some dead links, please let us know at: http://www.celebritylocator.com/

Marisa Tomei
http://www.marisa-tomei.org/

Lily Tomlin
http://www.lilytomlin.com/

John Travolta
http://www.travolta.com/

Peggy Trentini
http://www.peggytrentini.com/

Lana Turner
http://www.cmgww.com/stars/turner/

Barbara Tyson
http://www.barbara-tyson.com/

U _____ U

Tracey Ullman
http://www.highwired.com/tullman/

Skeet Ulrich
http://www.skeet.ulrich.com/skeet.html

Robert Urich
http://www.roberturich.com/

V _____ V

Paul Michael Valley
http://members.dencity.com/dramafan/pmvalley.html

Jean-Claude Van Damme
http://www.geocities.com/Hollywood/Academy/7928/index.html

James Van der Beek
http://members.tripod.com/~jvdb_/

Casper Van Dien
http://www.caspervandien.net/

If you find some dead links, please let us know at: http://www.celebritylocator.com/

Vince Vaughn
http://www.vincev.com/

Sofia Vergara
http://www.sofiavergara.com/

Ben Vereen
http://www.benvereen.com/

Asia Vieira
http://www.geocities.com/~dhdenney/asia/index.html

Adam Vignola
http://www.adamvignola.com/

Jenna von Oy
http://www.jennavonoy.com/

W   W

Natasha Gregson Wagner
http://www.best.com/~abacus/ngw/natasha.html

Robert Wagner
http://www.robert-wagner.com/

Denzel Washington
http://user.pa.net/~joelong/home.htm

Alberta Watson
http://www.albertawatson.com/

The Wayans Family
http://www.wayansfamily.com/

John Wayne
http://home.cdsnet.net/~lwood/wayne/wayne.htm

Steven Weber
http://www.geocities.com/Hollywood/Lot/7339/index.htm

Adam West
http://www.adamwest.com/

If you find some dead links, please let us know at: http://www.celebritylocator.com/

Mae West
http://www.maewest.net/

Lisa Whelchel
http://www.lisawhelchel.com/

Ester Williams
http://www.esther-williams.com/

Vanessa Williams
http://www.geocities.com/SunsetStrip/Studio/2139/

Bruce Willis
http://www.brucewillis.nu/

Bridgette Wilson
http://www.bridgette.person.dk/

Peta Wilson
http://www.petawilson.com/

Sheree J. Wilson
http://www.shereejwilson.com/

Oprah Winfrey
http://www.oprah.com

Kate Winslet
http://www.kate-winslet.org/

Elijah Wood
http://www.elijahwood.com/

Kari Wuhrer
http://www.kari-wuhrer.com/

Noah Wyle
http://www.btinternet.com/~orlando/wyle.htm

Victoria Wyndham
http://www.victoriawyndham.com/

If you find some dead links, please let us know at: http://www.celebritylocator.com/

Y   Y

Loretta Young
http://www.lorettayoung.com/

Anita Yuen
http://www.famouswomen.com/anita/anita.htm

Chow Yun-Fat
http://www.geocities.com/Athens/8907/factor.html

Z   Z

Renee Zellweger
http://www.townecryernews.com/

Catherine Zeta Jones
http://www.catherine-zetajones.com/

Zima Sisters
http://www.teleport.com/~patv/zimasis.htm

Stephanie Zimbalist
http://www.stephaniezimbalist.com/

If you find some dead links, please let us know at: http://www.celebritylocator.com/

Music

A _____ A

ABBA
http://abba.musichall.cz/

AC/DC
http://come.to/ACDC.com

Ace of Base
http://www.aceofbase.net/

Bryan Adams
http://www.bryanadams.com/

Aerosmith
http://www.aerosmith.com/

Alice In Chain
http://www.aliceinchains.com/

Allman Brothers
http://www.allmanbrothersband.com/

Tori Amos
http://www.toriamos.org/

Anathema
http://www.blackmetal.com/~mega/Anathema/

Adam Ant
http://www.adam-ant.net/

Leah Andreone
http://www.leahandreone.com/

Fiona Apple
http://www.fiona-apple.com/

Aqua
http://www.aqua.dk/

Archer/Park
http://www.traveller.com/archpark/

If you find some dead links, please let us know at: http://www.celebritylocator.com/

Arianna
http://www.ariannausa.com/

Louis Armstrong
http://www.louisarmstrong.org/

The Articles
http://www.thearticles.com/

Chet Atkins
http://www.chetatkins.com/

Atwater-Donnelly
http://members.aol.com/AubreyFolk/

B _____ **B**

Baby Snufkin
http://www.jibe.com/snufkin/

Johann Sebastian Bach
http://www.jsbach.org/

Bad Boy Entertainment
http://www.badboyonline.com/

Barenaked Ladies
http://www.bnl.org/

Cecilia Bartoli
http://www.cecilia-bartoli.com/

Beastie Boys
http://www.Beastieboys.com/

The Beatles
http://www.sonic.net/~custom/beat.html

Beck
http://www.beck-web.com/

Pat Benatar
http://www.benatar.com/

If you find some dead links, please let us know at: http://www.celebritylocator.com/

Matraca Berg
http://www.matraca.com

Hector Berlioz
http://home.earthlink.net/~oy/berlioz.html

Big Country
http://www.bigcountry.co.uk/

Big Head Todd & the Monsters
http://www.bigheadtodd.com/

Bjork
http://www.bjork.com/

Black Sabbath
http://www.black-sabbath.com/

Clint Black
http://www.clintblackfans.com/

Black Oak Arkansas
http://www.blackoakarkansas.com/

Blink-182
http://www.blink182.com/

Alpha Blondy
http://www.alphablondy.org/

Michael Bolton
http://www.michaelbolton.com/

Trace Bonham
http://www.TracyBonham.com/

Boom Shaka
http://www.boomshaka.com/

David Bowie
http://www.davidbowie.com/

BoyzIIMen
http://fanasylum.com/boyz2men/

If you find some dead links, please let us know at: http://www.celebritylocator.com/

Boyzone
http://www.boyzone.co.uk/

Delaney Bramlett
http://www.bluesparadise.com/delaney/

Brandy
http://www.foreverbrandy.com/

The Breeders
http://www.noaloha.com/

Brooks & Dunn
http://www.brooks-dunn.com/

Garth Brooks
http://www.garthbrooks.net/

Meredith Brooks
http://www.meredithbrooks.com/

Julie Brown
http://www.Julie-Brown.com/

Betty Buckley
http://www.bettybuckley.com/

Jeff Buckley
http://www.creednet.com/

Jimmy Buffett
http://www.cobo.org/

Solomon Burke
http://www.solomonburke.com/

David Burnham
http://www.davidburnham.com/

Bush
http://www.bushnet.com/home/

Butthole Surfers
http://www.buttholesurfers.com/

If you find some dead links, please let us know at: http://www.celebritylocator.com/

C   C

Cake
http://www.cakemusic.com/

Maria Callas
http://www.callas.it/

Camel
http://www.inertron.com/camel/

Candlebox
http://www.candlebox.com/

Canibus
http://www.canibus.com/

Canned Heat
http://www.cannedheatmusic.com/

Freddy Cannon
http://www.freddycannon.com/

Mariah Carey
http://www.mariahcarey.com/

Benny Carter
http://www.bennycarter.com/

Johnny Cash
http://www.johnnycash.com/

David Cassidy
http://www.davidcassidy.com/

Tracy Chapman
http://www.tracychapman.net/

Ray Charles
http://www.raycharles.com/

Charo
http://www.charo.com/

If you find some dead links, please let us know at: http://www.celebritylocator.com/

Chayanne
http://www.chayanne.net/

The Chemical Brothers
http://www.astralwerks.com/chemical/

Cher
http://www.Cher.com/

Cherry Poppin' Daddies
http://www.netsedge.com/daddies/

Chicago
http://www.chirecords.com/

Coal Chamber
http://www.coalchamber.com/

Eric Clapton
http://www.slowhand.net/

Leonard Cohen
http://www.leonardCohen.com/

Steve Coleman
http://www.m-base.com/

Judy Collins
http://www.judycollins.com/

Shawn Colvin
http://www.shawncolvin.com/

Commander Cody
http://www.commandercody.com/

Harry Connick, Jr.
http://www.connick.com/

Larry Coryell
http://www.kiosek.com/coryell/

Elvis Costello
http://www.elvis-costello.com/

If you find some dead links, please let us know at: http://www.celebritylocator.com/

Cowboy Junkies
http://www.cowboyjunkies.com/

The Cranberries
http://www.cranberries.ie/

Counting Crows
http://www.countingcrows.com/

Crash Test Dummies
http://www.crashtestdummies.com/

Crosby, Stills & Nash
http://www.crosbystillsnash.com/

Christopher Cross
http://www.christophercross.com/

Sheryl Crow
http://www.sherylcrow.com/

The Cure
http://www.thecure.com/

D   D

Mark Dacascos
http://dacascos.com/

Dick Dale
http://www.dickdale.com/

Charlie Daniels
http://www.charliedaniels.com/

Bobby Darin
http://www.bobbydarin.net/

Ray Davies
http://www.raydavies.com/

Miles Davis
http://www.milesdavis.com/

If you find some dead links, please let us know at: http://www.celebritylocator.com/

DC Talk
http://www.ardent-enthusiast.com/

Dead Man's Curve
http://www.jukebox.demon.co.uk/

Billy Dean
http://www.billydean.com/

Deftones
http://www.deftones.com/

Depeche Mode
http://www.depeche-mode.com/

Rick Derringer
http://www.rickderringer.com/

Al Di Meola
http://www.aldimeola.com/

The Dixie Chicks
http://www.DixieChicks.com/

Ani Diffranco
http://www.anidifranco.net/

Celine Dion
http://www.celineonline.com/

Placido Domingo
http://www.placidodomingo.com/

The Doors
http://www.the-doors.com/

Dr. Dre
http://wallofsound.go.com/artists/drdre/home.html

Duran Duran
http://www.duranduran.com/

Bob Dylan
http://www.bobdylan.com/

If you find some dead links, please let us know at: http://www.celebritylocator.com/

E   E

Eagle
http://badger.ac.brocku.ca/~bi95aa/sadcafe.html

Bobbie Eakes
http://www.bobbieeakes.com/

Earth, Wind & Fire
http://www.earthwindandfire.com/

Madeline Eastman
http://www.madelineeastman.com/

Sheena Easton
http://www.sheenaeaston.com/

Duke Ellington
http://duke.fuse.net/

Joe Ely
http://www.ely.com/

Eminem
http://www.eminem.com/

Enigma
http://www.enigma3.com/

Peter Erskine
http://petererskine.com/

Gloria Estefan
http://www.epiccenter.com/EpicCenter/custom/56/

Melissa Etheridge
http://www.melissaetheridge.com/

Eve 6
http://www.eve6.com/

F _____ F

Maynard Ferguson
http://www.maynardferguson.com/

Melissa Ferrick
http://www.melissaferrick.com/

Ferron
http://ferronweb.com/

First Church Of Chumbawamba
http://www.chumba.com/

Fleetwood Mac
http://www.fleetwoodmac.net/

John Fogerty
http://www.johnfogerty.com/

Frankie Ford
http://www.frankieford.com/

Vivica Fox
http://www.vivicafox.com/

Peter Frampton
http://www.frampton.com/

Aretha Franklin
http://webhome.globalserve.net/ebutler

G _____ G

Peter Gabriel
http://www.petergabriel.com/

Garbage
http://www.garbage.com/

Jerry Garcia
http://www.dead.net/

If you find some dead links, please let us know at: http://www.celebritylocator.com/

Genesis
http://www.genesis.com/

Vince Gill
http://www.vincegill.com/

Goo Goo Dolls
http://www.GooGooDolls.com/

Lesley Gore
http://listen.to/lesley

Graham Central Station
http://www.gcsweb.org/

Amy Grant
http://www.amygrant.com/

Grateful Dead
http://www.dead.net/

Dobie Gray
http://www.dobiegray.com/

Green Day
http://www.greenday.net/

Casey Lee Green
http://www.caseyleegreen.com/

Grooverider
http://www.grooverider.com/

The Gumbi Band
http://www.thegumbiband.com/

Guns N' Roses
http://www.bzzt.com/gnrbar/

Buddy Guy
http://www.buddyguys.com/

H _____ H

Charlie Haden
http://interjazz.com/haden/

Loretta Hagen
http://www.LorettaHagen.com/

Merle Haggard
http://www.merlehaggard.com/

Hall & Oates
http://www.hallandoates.com/

Hanson
http://hansonline.com/

George Harrison
http://www.georgeharrison.com/

Deborah Harry
http://www.primenet.com/~lab/deborahharry.html

PJ Harvey
http://www.pjharvey.net/

Ronnie Hawkins
http://www.pipcom.com/~thehawk/index.html

Isaac Hayes
http://www.isaachayes.com/

Hepcat
http://www.iration.com/hepcat/

Hieroglyphics
http://www.hieroglyphics.com/

Faith Hill
http://www.faithhill.com/
(another Faith Hill site)
http://www.wbr.com/faithhill/

Tish Hinojosa
http://www.wbr.com/tishhinojosa/

Hiroshima
http://www.hiroshimamusic.com/

Hit Me !!
http://www.hitme.net/

Whitney Houston
http://www.classicwhitney.com/

I _____ I

Ice Cube
http://www.icecube.com/

Iced Earth
http://www.icedearth.com/

Natalie Imbruglia
http://www.imbruglia.com/

Indigo Girls
http://www.IndigoGirls.com/
(another Indigo Girls site)
http://www.epiccenter.com/EpicCenter/IndigoGirls/

Julio Iglesias, Jr.
http://www.Julioiglesias.com/

Insane Clown Posse
http://www.insaneclownposse.com/

INXS
http://www.inxs.com/

Iron Butterfly
http://www.ironbutterfly.com/

J _____ J

Alan Jackson
http://www.alanjackson.com/

Irene Jackson
http://www.irenejackson.com/

Janet Jackson
http://www.janetjackson.com/
(another Janet Jackson site)
http://www.janet.nu/

Joe Jackson
http://www.joejackson.com/
(another Joe Jackson
http://www.jj-archive.net/

Michael Jackson
http://www.mjifc.com/

Jana Jae
http://www.janajae.com/

Tommy James
http://www.tommyjames.com/

Jamiroquai
http://www.jamiroquai.co.uk/jamiroquai/

Jane's Addiction
http://www.janesaddiction.com/

Jars of Clay
http://www.jarsofclay.com/

Jay-Z
http://listen.to/jay-z

Wyclef Jean
http://www.wyclef.com/wyclefindex.html

If you find some dead links, please let us know at: http://www.celebritylocator.com/

Jewel
http://jeweljk.com/

Billy Joel
http://www.billyjoel.com/

Elton John
http://eltonjohn.com/

Al Jolson
http://www.jolson.org/

Quincy Jones
http://www.duke.edu/~jcf3/

Journey
http://www.journey-tribute.com/

Tom Joyner
http://www.tomjoyner.com/

Ashley Judd
http://twomoons.simplenet.com/thealtar/

K   K

Mike Keneally
http://www.keneally.com/

KerbStar
http://www.krebstar.com/

Chaka Khan
http://www.chakakhan.com/

Angelique Kidjo
http://wwwusers.imaginet.fr/~kidjo/

Kill Creek
http://www.killcreek.com/

B.B. King
http://www.bbking.com/

The King's Singers
http://www.singers.com/kings.html

The Kinks
http://kinks.it.rit.edu/

Kiss
http://KissAsylum.com

KMFDM
http://www.kmfdm.net/

David Knopfler
http://www.knopfler.com/

Korn
http://www.korn.com/

Lenny Kravitz
http://www.lennykravitz.com/

Krs-One
http://www.peeps.com/krs-one/

Ruriko Kuboh
http://www.sentex.net/~sardine/ruriko.html

Ed Kuepper
http://server.tt.net/hot/kuepper/

L _____ L

Ladysmith Black Mambazo
http://www.mambazo.com/

Greg Lake
http://www.greglake.com/

k. d. Lang
http://www.kdlang.com/
(another k. d. Lang site)
http://www.wbr.com/kdlang/

If you find some dead links, please let us know at: http://www.celebritylocator.com/

David Lanz
http://www.davidlanz.com/

Terry Larch
http://members.tripod.com/~larch/index.html

Led Zeppelin
http://www.led-zeppelin.com/

Sonny Boy Lee
http://www.sonnyboylee.com/

Richard Leech
http://www.richardleech.com/

Legendary Pink Dots
http://www.brainwashed.com/lpd/

Danni Leigh
http://www.dannileigh.com/

Julian Lennon
http://www.julianlennon.com/
(another Julian Lenno site)
http://www.geocities.com/Hollywood/Boulevard/2801/index.html

Brad Little
http://www.bradlittle.com/

Loverboy
http://members.xoom.com/theluckyones/

Mark Lowry
http://www.marklowry.com/

Lucky Dude
http://www.luckydube.com/

Lynyrd Skynyrd
http://www.skynyrd.com/

M _____ M

Rita MacNeil
http://www.ritamacneil.com/

Madness
http://www.madness.co.uk/

Madonna
http://www.madonnanet.com/
(another Madonna site)
http://www.wbr.com/madonna/

Malaika
http://www.malaika.ca/

Man...or Astro-man?
http://www.astroman.com/

Manhattan Brass Quintet
http://www.quicklink.com/~antman/MBQ/

Manic Street Preachers
http://www.manics.co.uk/

Barry Manilow
http://www.manilow.com/

Andrea Marcovicci
http://www.marcovicci.com

Marcy Playground
http://www.marcyplayground.com/

Kitty Margolis
http://www.kittymargolis.com/

Marillion
http://www.marillion.com/

Marilyn Manson
http://www.marilynmanson.net/

If you find some dead links, please let us know at: http://www.celebritylocator.com/

Marky Mark
http://www.markymark.com/

Bob Marley
http://www.bobmarley.com/
(another Bob Marley site)
http://www.niceup.com/marley.html

Ziggy Marley
http://www.ziggymarley.com

Richard Marx
http://www.richardmarx.com/

Dana Mase
http://www.danamase.com/

Massive Attack
http://the-raft.com/massive/index.html

MasterP
http://masterp.org/

Matchbox 20
http://www.matchbox20.com/
(another Matchbox 20 site)
http://www.geocities.com/SunsetStrip/Backstage/1135/

Dave Matthews Band
http://www.dmband.com/

Max Creek
http://www.maxcreek.com/

Martina McBride
http://www.martina-mcbride.com/

Paul McCartney
http://www.paulmccartney.com/
(another Paul McCartney site)
http://www.mplcommunications.com/mccartney/

Mindy McCready
http://www.mindymccready.com/

Martine McCutcheon
http://www.martinemccutcheon.com/

Reba McEntire
http://www.reba.com/

Bobby McFerrin
http://www.bobbymcferrin.com

Maureen McGovern
http://www.maureenmcgovern.com/

Tim McGraw
http://www.timmcgraw.com/

Sarah McLachlan
http://www.sarahmclachlan.com/

Mighty Sam Mclain
http://www.mightysam.com/

Meat Loaf
http://www.1webplaza.com/meatloaf.html

Medeski, Martin & Wood
http://www.mmw.net/

John Mellencamp
http://www.mellencamp.com/

Melon Patch
http://www.melonpatch.com/

Men out Loud
http://www.menoutloud.com/

Natalie Merchant
http://www.nataliemerchant.com/

Freddie Mercury
http://www.webring.org/cgi-bin/webring?ring=freddiering&list

Metallica
http://www.metallica.com/
(another Metallica site)
http://www.metclub.com/

Pat Metheny
http://www.pat-metheny.com

Method Man
http://www.defjam.com/artists/method/method.html

George Michael
http://www.georgemichael.net/
(another George Michael site)
http://www.ozemail.com.au/~alhatu/gm.htm

Bette Midler
http://www.wbr.com/bettemidler/

Mighty Mighty Bosstones
http://www.geocities.com/SunsetStrip/Towers/6931/

Charles Mingus
http://www.mingusmingusmingus.com/

Liza Minnelli
http://www.lizamay.com/

Dannii Minoque
http://www.dannii.com/

Miss Elliott
http://www.missy-elliott.com/

Joni Mitchell
http://www.jonimitchell.com/

Moby
http://www.moby.org/

If you find some dead links, please let us know at: http://www.celebritylocator.com/

Katy Moffatt
http://www.katymoffatt.com

T.S. Monk
http://www.jazzcorner.com/monk.html

The Monkees
http://www.monkees.net/

Moody Blues
http://www.moodyblues.co.uk/

Lorrie Morgan
http://www.Lorrie.com

Alanis Morissette
http://www.alanismorissette.net/

Van Morrison
http://www.harbour.sfu.ca/~hayward/van/van.html

Motley Crue
http://www.motley.com/

Mott the Hoople
http://www.hunter-mott.com/

Mudhoney
http://www.unofficial-mudhoney.com/

David Lee Murphy
http://www.davidleemurphy.com/

Charles Musselwhite
http://www.rosebudus.com/musselwhite/

N _____ **N**

N' Sync
http://www.nsync.com/

David Nelson Band
http://www.nelsonband.com/

If you find some dead links, please let us know at: http://www.celebritylocator.com/

Willie Nelson
http://www.willienelson.com/

Michael Nesmith
http://www.videoranch.com/
(another Michael Nesmith site)
http://198.49.210.81/nesmith.asp

New Kids On The Block
http://www.nkotb.com/

Wayne Newton
http://www.waynenewton.net/

Olivia Newton-John
http://www.onlyolivia.com/onj.html

Nirvana
http://pw1.netcom.com/~dperle/nirvana/nirvlinks.html

Nitty Gritty Dirt Band
http://www.nittygritty.com/

No Doubt
http://www.nodoubt.com/

Notorious B.I.G.
http://www.notoriousbig.com/
(another Notorious B.I.G. site)
http://www.geocities.com/NapaValley/4035/big.html

Ted Nugent
http://www.tednugent.com

Steve Nystrup
http://www.xenonarts.com/music/nystrup/index.html

O _____ **O**

Oak Ridge Boys
http://www.oakridgeboys.com/

If you find some dead links, please let us know at: http://www.celebritylocator.com/

Oasis
http://www.oasisinet.com/

Ocean Colour Scene
http://www.oceancolourscene.com/

Sinead O'Connor
http://www.sinead-oconnor.com/

Offspring
http://www.offspring.com/

Oingo Boingo
http://www.oingoboingo.com/

Mike Oldfield
http://tubular.net/

Omar & The Howlers
http://www.drfeelgood.de/omar/index.htm

Once Hush
http://www.oncehush.com/

The Orb
http://www.theorb.com/

Joan Osborne
http://www.joanosborne.com/
(another Joan Osborne site)
http://users.aol.com/drldeboer2/htm/jo.htm

Ozzy Osbourne
http://www.ozzyosbourne.com/
(another Ozzy Osbourne site)
http://www.ozzynet.com/

Donny Osmond
http://www.donny.com/

Marie Osmond
http://www.osmond.com/marie/

The Osmonds
http://www.osmond.com/
(another Osmonds site)
http://www.osmond.net/

The Outhere Brothers
http://www.masscot.com/aureus/outhere.html

P _____ P

Pantera
http://www.vdopantera.com/

Jon Kimura Parker
http://www.kimura.com/

Gram Parsons
http://www.gramparsons.com/

Dolly Parton
http://www.Dollywood.com/

Luciano Pavarotti
http://www.lucianopavarotti.it/

Pavement
http://www.slip.net/~pavement/

Pearl Jam
http://www.pearljam.com/
(another Pearl Jam site)
http://www.fivehorizons.com/

Pessimist Black Death Metal
http://www.sting-ray.com/pessimist/

Michael Peterson
http://www.michaelpeterson.com/

Pet Shop Boys
http://www.petshopboys.com/

If you find some dead links, please let us know at: http://www.celebritylocator.com/

Tom Petty
http://www.tompetty.com/

Liz Phair
http://www.lizphair.com/

Phish
http://www.phish.com/

Pink Floyd
http://www.pinkfloyd.com/

Pixies
http://www.ozemail.com.au/~thrashin/pixies.htm

The Platters
http://www.theplatters.com/

Poi Dog Pondering
http://www.poidogpondering.com/

Point of Grace
http://www.wordrecords.com/pog/

Jean-Luc Ponty
http://www.ponty.com/

Iggy Pop
http://www.iggypop.org/

Portishead
http://www.portishead.co.uk/

Elvis Presley
http://www.elvis.com/

Gary Primich
http://www.garyprimich.com/
(another Gary Primich site)
http://www.drfeelgood.de/primich/index.htm

Primus
http://www.primussucks.com/

If you find some dead links, please let us know at: http://www.celebritylocator.com/

Prince (formely known)
http://www.love4oneanother.com/

Prodigy
http://www.prodigy.co.uk/

Psychobilly
http://www.wreckingpit.com/

Giacomo Puccini
http://www.puccini.it/

Puff Daddy
http://www.badboyonline.com/

Q _____ **Q**

Queen
http://queen-fip.com/

Queensryche
http://www.queensryche.com/

R _____ **R**

Radiohead
http://www.radiohead.com/

Rage Against The Machine
http://www.ratm.com/

Bonnie Raitt
http://www.bonnieraitt.com/
(another Bonnie Raitt site)
http://home.worldonline.nl/~dalmeier/bonnie.htm

Rammstein
http://www.rammstein.com/

The Ramones
http://www.kauhajoki.fi/~jplaitio/ramones.html

Collin Raye
http://collinraye.com/

Red Hot Chili Peppers
http://www.redhotchilipeppers.com/

Red House Painters
http://www.kdesigns.com/rhp/

Lou Reed
http://www.loureed.org/

Cliff Richard
http://www.cliffrichard.com/
(another Cliff Richard site)
http://www.sir-cliff.com/

LeAnn Rimes
http://www.rimestimes.com/
(another LeAnn Rime site)
http://www.leannrimes.com/

Majel Roddenberry
http://www.roddenberry.com/

Tommy Roe
http://www.tommyroe.com/

The Rolling Stones
http://www.stones.net/
(another Rolling Stones site)
http://www.angelfire.com/pa/redlands/links.html

RUSH
http://www.r-u-s-h.com/

Tom Rush
http://www.tomrush.com/

Jeri Lynn Ryan
http://www.jerilynn.com/

Shayna Ryan
http://www.shaynamania.com/

If you find some dead links, please let us know at: http://www.celebritylocator.com/

Bobby Rydell
http://www.bobbyrydell.com/

S _____ **S**

Melanie Safka
http://web.inter.nl.net/users/dj/melanie/

Buffy Saint-Marie
http://hookomo.aloha.net/~bsm/

Carlos Santana
http://www.santana.com/

Joe Satriani
http://www.satriani.com/

Savage Garden
http://www.savagegarden.com/main.html

Savatage
http://www.savatage.com/

Seal
http://www.wbr.com/seal/index.html

Brady Seals
http://bradyseals.com/

Sebadoh
http://www.sebadoh.com/
(another Sebadoh site)
http://www.subpop.com/bands/sebadoh/website/

See Jane Run
http://www.seejanerun.com/

Bob Seger
http://www.execpc.com/~pblock/seger.html

Sex Pistols
http://www.sexpistols.org

If you find some dead links, please let us know at: http://www.celebritylocator.com/

Sha Na Na
http://www.shanana.com/

Tupac Shakur
http://www.tupacshakur.com/
(another Tupac Shakur site)
http://www.tupacfans.com/

Kevin Sharp
http://www.kevinsharp.com/

Vonda Shepard
http://www.vesperalley.com/

Silverchair
http://www.chairpage.com/

Frank Sinatra
http://www.franksinatra.com/

Sly & Family Stone
http://www.slyfamstone.com/

Smashing Pumpkins
http://www.smashingpumpkins.com/
(another Smashing Pumpkins site)
http://www.netphoria.org/

Patti Smith
http://www.phtp.com/

Snoop Doggy Dogg
http://www.snoopdogg.com/

Son Volt
http://www.wbr.com/SonVolt/

Soundgarden
http://imusic.artistdirect.com/soundgarden/

Britney Spears
http://www.britneyspears.com/

If you find some dead links, please let us know at: http://www.celebritylocator.com/

(anoiher Britney Spears site)
http://surf.to/britneyspears

Torri Spelling
http://www.tori-spelling.com/

Spice Girls
http://www.spicegirls.org/
(another Spice Girls site)
http://www.angelfire.com/ny/spicelinks/index.html

Spinal Tap
http://www.spinaltap.com/

Bruce Springsteen
http://www.brucespringsteen.com/

http://members.xoom.com/M_Steinegger/bruce.html

Squirrel Nut Zippers
http://www.snzippers.com/

Ringo Starr
http://www.ringotour.com/

Steely Dan
http://www.steelydan.com/

Rod Stewart
http://www.rodstewartlive.com/

Ray Stevens
http://www.raystevens.com/

Sting
http://www.sting.com/

Gale Storm
http://members.nbci.com/ajrfman/GaleStorm2.html

George Strait
http://www.georgestrait.com/

If you find some dead links, please let us know at: http://www.celebritylocator.com/

Barbra Streisand
http://www.barbrastreisand.com/

Suede
http://www.suede.net/

Yma Sumac
http://www.accesscom.com/~pc/sumac/

Andy Summers
http://www.andysummers.com/

T _____ **T**

Talking Heads
http://www.talking-heads.net/

Ken Tamplin
http://www.kentamplin.com/

James Taylor
http://www.james-taylor.com/

Teenage Fanclub
http://www.teenagefanclub.com/

The Tenison Twins
http://www.tenisontwins.com/

John Tesh
http://www.tesh.com/

They Might Be Giants
http://www.tmbg.com/

Third Eye Blind
http://www.3eb.com/

Tiffany
http://www.tiffany.org/

TLC
http://www.Geocities.com/Hollywood/2320/

If you find some dead links, please let us know at: http://www.celebritylocator.com/

Peter Tork
http://www.petertork.com

Toto
http://www.toto99.com/

Randy Travis
http://www.randy-travis.com/

Gloria Trevi
http://www.trevi.com/

Travis Tritt
http://www.travis-tritt.com/

Marshall Tucker Band
http://www.marshalltucker.com/

Tina Turner
http://www.Tina-Turner.com/

Shania Twain
http://www.shania.com/

U   U

U2
http://zoonation.com/indexB.html

Ulali
http://www.ulali.com/

V   V

Steve Vaile
http://www.stevevaile.com

Steve Ray Vaughan
http://www.srvfanclub.com/

Suzanne Vega
http://www.vega.net/

If you find some dead links, please let us know at: http://www.celebritylocator.com/

Velvet Chain
http://www.velvetchain.com//

Vigilantes of Love
http://www.coaster.com/VOL/

Violent Femmes
http://www.vfemmes.com/

W _____ W

Fates Warning
http://www.fateswarning.com/

Wet Willie
http://www.ktb.net/~insync/wet_willie.html

Ian Whitcomb
http://www.ianwhitcomb.com

Sonny Boy Williams II
http://www.sonnyboy.com/

Nancy Wilson (Heart)
http://www.annandnancy.com/

Johnny Winter
http://members.tripod.com/~Plaza_Mike/links.html

Steve Winwood
http://www.stevewinwood.com/

Chely Wright
http://www.chely.com/

X _____ X

Xuxa
http://www.xuxa.com.br/

If you find some dead links, please let us know at: http://www.celebritylocator.com/

Y _____ Y

Weird Al Yankovic
http://www.weirdal.com/

Yanni
http://www.yanni.com/

Trisha Yearwood
http://www.totallytrisha.com/

Yes
http://www.yesmag.com/

Yothu Yindi
http://www.yothuyindi.com/

Dwight Yoakam
http://www.dwightyoakam.net/

Kathleen York
http://www.kathleenyork.com/

Young Dubliners
http://www.youngdubs.com/new.html

The Young Gods
http://www.theyounggods.com/

Neil Young
http://www.neilyoung.com/
(another Neil Young site)
http://www.hyperrust.org/

Z _____ Z

Frank Zappa
http://www.zappa.com/

ZZ Top
http://www.zztop.com/

If you find some dead links, please let us know at: http://www.celebritylocator.com/

Sports

A _____ A

Helen Alfredsson
http://www.algonet.se/~gulthus/helen/index.htm

Andrea Agassi
http://www.andresite.com/

Bobb Allison
http://www.bobbyallison.com/

B _____ B

Oksana Baiul
http://www.baiul.org/

Yogi Berra
http://www.yogiberra.com/

Shae-Lynn Bourne
http://www.skate.org/b+k/

Isabelle Brasseur
http://www.skate.org/b+e/

Kurt Browning
http://www.skate.org/browning/

Mark Brunell
http://www.mark-brunell.com/

C _____ C

Michael Chang
http://www.mchang.com/

Ben Crenshaw
http://www.bencrenshaw.com/

If you find some dead links, please let us know at: http://www.celebritylocator.com/

D

John Daly
http://www.gripitandripit.com/

Oscar DeLahoya
http://www.oscardelahoya.com/

E

Lloyd Eisler
http://www.skate.org/b+e/

F

Melissa Ferrick
http://www.best.com/~kluce/mf.htm

Raymond Floyd
http://www.rayfloyd.com/

George Foreman
http://www.georgeforeman.com/

G

Ekaterina Gordeeva
http://www.fred.net/paula/katia.html

Jeff Gordon
http://www.jeffgordon.com/

H

Scott Hamilton
http://members.aol.com/revjoelle/index.html

Anita Hartshorn
http://www.fred.net/paula/hart.html

If you find some dead links, please let us know at: http://www.celebritylocator.com/

Grant Hill
http://www.granthill.com/

Evander Holyfield
http://www.evanderholyfield.com/

Christine Hough
http://www.skate.org/h+l/

J _____ **J**

Michael Jordan
http://jordan.sportsline.com/

K _____ **K**

Anna Kournikova
http://www.annakournikova.com/

Victor Kraatz
http://www.skate.org/b+k/

Michelle Kwan
http://members.tripod.com/~themksite/index.html

L _____ **L**

Doug Ladret
http://www.skate.org/h+l/

Tara Lipinski
http://www.taralipinski.com/

Chen Lu
http://www.skate.org/chen/

M _____ **M**

Elizabeth Manley
http://www.skate.org/manley/

If you find some dead links, please let us know at: http://www.celebritylocator.com/

Diego Armando Maradona
http://www.diegomaradona.com

Paul Martini
http://www.skate.org/u+m/

Don Mattingly
http://www.don-mattingly.com/

Michelle McGann
http://www.geocities.com/Wellesley/2526/

Willie McGee
http://www.williemcgee.com/

Phil Mickelson

Joe Montana
http://www.joemontanafanclub.com/

N _____ **N**

Greg Norman
http://www.gregnorman.com/
(another Greg Norma site)
http://www.shark.com/

O _____ **O**

Shaquille O'Neal
http://www.shaq.com/

Brian Orser
http://www.skate.org/orser/

P _____ **P**

Satchel Paige
http://www.cmgww.com/baseball/paige/paige.html

If you find some dead links, please let us know at: http://www.celebritylocator.com/

Gary Payton
http://www.inficad.com/~treyman7/index.html

R　　　　　　　　　　　　　　　　　　　　　R

Jerry Rice
http://www.jerryrice.net/

David Robinson
http://www.theadmiral.com/

Dennis Rodman
http://lonestar.texas.net/~pmagal/

Pete Rose
http://www.peterose.com/

Babe Ruth
http://www.baberuth.com/
(another Babe Ruth site)
http://www.baberuthmuseum.com/

S　　　　　　　　　　　　　　　　　　　　　S

Jozef Sabovcik
http://www3.islandnet.com/~luree/joe/jozef.html

Pete Sampras
http://www.petesampras.com/

Monica Seles
http://www.monicaseles.org/

Daniel Shank
http://www.ismi.net/~joemill/shank.htm

Elvis Stojko
http://heartofgold.topcities.com/

Ozzie Smith
http://www.ozziesmith.com/

If you find some dead links, please let us know at: http://www.celebritylocator.com/

U

Barbara Underhill
http://www.skate.org/u+m/

V

Mo Vaughn
http://www.geocities.com/Colosseum/Track/4242/

W

Ted Williams
http://www.tedwilliams.com/

Serena Williams
http://www.venusserenafans.com/

Venus Williams
http://www.venusserenafans.com/

Katarina Witt
http://www.katarinawitt.de/

Tiger Woods
http://www.tigerwoods.com/

Paul Wylie
http://www.geocities.com/Colosseum/Arena/1736/

Y

Kristi Yamaguchi
http://promotions.yahoo.com/promotions/kristi/

Carl Yastrzemski
http://www.carlyastrzemski.com/
(another Carl Yastrzemski site)
http://home.epix.net/~brett/yaz.html

If you find some dead links, please let us know at: http://www.celebritylocator.com/

Politics

A   A

Rep. Bill Archer (TX)
http://www.house.gov/archer/

Rep. Dick Armey (TX)
http://armey.house.gov/

John Ashcroft
http://www.usdoj.gov/ag/index.html

B   B

Sec. Bruce Babbitt
http://www.doi.gov/secretary/index.html

Sen. Evan Bayh
http://www.senate.gov/~bayh/

Sen. Joseph A. Biden (DL)
http://www.senate.gov/~biden/

P.M. Tony Blair
http://www.number-10.gov.uk/

Rep. David Bonior (MI)
http://davidbonior.house.gov/

Rep. Mary Bono (CA)
http://www.house.gov/bono/

Sen. Barbara Boxer
http://www.senate.gov/~boxer/

Sen. John Breaux (LA)
http://www.senate.gov/~breaux/

Rep. George Brown (CA)
http://www.house.gov/georgebrown/

Sen. Richard Bryan (NV)
http://www.senate.gov/~bryan/

If you find some dead links, please let us know at: http://www.celebritylocator.com/

Sen. Jim Bunning (KY)
http://www.senate.gov/~bunning/

Sen. Conrad Burns (MT)
http://www.senate.gov/~burns/

George W. Bush, Jr.
http://www.whitehouse.gov/president/

Gov. Jed Bush (FL)
http://www.state.fl.us/eog/

Laura Welch Bush
http://www.whitehouse.gov/president/flbio.html

Sen. Robert Byrd (WA)
http://www.senate.gov/~byrd/

C _____ C

Sen. Ben Campbell (CO)
http://www.senate.gov/~campbell/

Gov. Paul Cellucci (MA)
http://www.state.ma.us/gov/gov.htm

Sen. John Chafee (FL)
http://www.senate.gov/~chafee/

Prince Charles
http://www.princeofwales.gov.uk/

Lynn V. Cheney
http://www.whitehouse.gov/president/mcbio.html

V.P. Richard B. Cheney
http://www.whitehouse.gov/president/vpbio.html

President Bill Clinton
http://www.clintonpresidentialcenter.com/

Hillary Rodhan-Clinton
http://clinton.senate.gov/

If you find some dead links, please let us know at: http://www.celebritylocator.com/

Sen. Thad Cochran (MS)
http://www.senate.gov/~cochran/

William S. Cohen
http://www.defenselink.mil/pubs/almanac/osd.html

Sen. Kent Conrad (ND)
http://www.senate.gov/~conrad/

Rep. John Conyers (MI)
http://www.house.gov/conyers/

Sen. Paul Coverdell (GA)
http://www.senate.gov/~coverdell/

Sen. Larry Craig (ID)
http://www.senate.gov/~craig/

Rep. Phillip Crane (IL)
http://www.house.gov/crane/

Andrew Cuomo
http://www.hud.gov/news/index.cfm

D   D

William Daley
http://www.osec.doc.gov/

Sen. Tom Daschle (SD)
http://www.senate.gov/~daschle/

Gov. Gary Davis (CA)
http://www.state.ca.us/s/

Sen. Mike DeWine (OH)
http://www.senate.gov/~dewine/

Princess Diana
http://www.royal.gov.uk/start.htm

Rep. John D. Dingell (MI)
http://www.house.gov/dingell/

If you find some dead links, please let us know at: http://www.celebritylocator.com/

Sen. Christopher Dobb (CT)
http://www.senate.gov/~dodd/

Sen. Pete Domenici (NM)
http://www.senate.gov/~domenici/

E _____ **E**

Queen Elizabeth II
http://www.royal.gov.uk/

Gov. John Engler (MI)
http://www.migov.state.mi.us/migov.html

Donald Evans
http://www.osec.doc.gov/

F _____ **F**

Sen. Russell Feingold (WI)
http://www.senate.gov/~feingold/

Sen. Dianne Feinstein (CA)
http://www.senate.gov/~feinstein/

Rep. Barney Frank (MA)
http://www.house.gov/frank/

G _____ **G**

Rep. Richard Gephardt (MO)
http://www.house.gov/gephardt/

Dan Glickman
http://www.usda.gov/agencies/gallery/glickman.htm

Sen. Slade Gorton (WA)
http://www.senate.gov/~gorton/

Sen. Bob Graham (FL)
http://www.senate.gov/~graham/

If you find some dead links, please let us know at: http://www.celebritylocator.com/

Sen. Phil Gramm (TX)
http://www.senate.gov/~gramm/

Sen. Charles Grassley (IA)
http://www.senate.gov/~grassley/

Alan Greenspan
http://www.federalreserve.gov/bios/Greenspan.htm

Sen. Judd Gregg (NH)
http://www.senate.gov/~gregg/

H   H

Sen. Chuck Hagert (NE)
http://www.senate.gov/~hagel/

Sen. Tom Harkin (IA)
http://www.senate.gov/~harkin/

Rep. Alcee L. Hastings (FL)
http://www.house.gov/alceehastings/

Sen. Orrin G. Hatch (UT)
http://www.senate.gov/~hatch/

Sen. Jesse Helms (NC)
http://www.senate.gov/~helms/

Alexis M. Herman
http://www.dol.gov/dol/opa/public/sec/secbio.htm

Sen. Fritz Hollings (SC)
http://www.senate.gov/~hollings/

Sen. Kay Bailey Hutchison (TX)
http://www.senate.gov/~hutchison/

Rep. Henry Hyde (IL)
http://www.house.gov/hyde/

Rep. Asa Hutchins (AR)
http://www.house.gov/hutchinson/

J _____ **J**

Sen. Tim Jeffords (VT)
http://www.senate.gov/~jeffords/

Sen. Tim Johnson (SD)
http://www.senate.gov/~johnson/

K _____ **K**

Anthony Kennedy
http://www.bowdoin.edu/~sbodurt2/court/kennedy.html

Sen. Edward Kennedy (MA)
http://www.senate.gov/~kennedy/

Rep. Patrick Kennedy (RI)
http://www.house.gov/patrickkennedy/

Sen. Robert Kerrey (NE)
http://www.senate.gov/~kerrey/

Sen. John Kerry (MA)
http://www.senate.gov/~kerry/

Sen. Jon Kyl (AZ)
http://www.senate.gov/~kyl/

L _____ **L**

Sen. Mary Landrieu (LA)
http://www.senate.gov/~landrieu/

Rep. Tom Lantos (CA)
http://www.house.gov/lantos/

Rep. Steve Largent (OK)
http://www.house.gov/largent/

If you find some dead links, please let us know at: http://www.celebritylocator.com/

Sen. Frank Lautenberg (NJ)
http://www.senate.gov/~lautenberg/

Rep. Jim Leach (IA)
http://www.house.gov/leach/

Sen. Patrick Leahy (VT)
http://www.senate.gov/~leahy/

Sen. Carl Levin (MI)
http://www.senate.gov/~levin/

Rep. John Lewis (GA)
http://www.house.gov/johnlewis/welcome.html

Sen. Joseph Lieberman (CT)
http://www.senate.gov/~lieberman/

Sen. Trent Lott (MS)
http://www.senate.gov/~lott/

Sen. Richard Lugar (IN)
http://www.senate.gov/~lugar/

M _____ M

Sen. Connie Mack (FL)
http://www.senate.gov/~mack/

Sec. Mel Martinez
http://www.hud.gov/news/index.cfm

Sen. John McCain (AZ)
http://www.senate.gov/~mccain/

Rep. Bill McCollum (FL)
http://www.house.gov/mccollum/

Sen. Mitch McConnell (KY)
http://www.senate.gov/~mcconnell/

Rep. Cynyhia McKinney (GA)
http://www.house.gov/mckinney/

If you find some dead links, please let us know at: http://www.celebritylocator.com/

Sen. Barbara A. Mikulski (MD)
http://www.senate.gov/~mikulski/

Sec. Norman Y. Mineta
http://www.dot.gov/affairs/mineta.htm

Rep. Patsy T. Mink (HI)
http://www.house.gov/mink/

Sen. Daniel Patrick Moynihan (NY)
http://www.senate.gov/~moynihan/

Sen. Frank Murkowski (AK)
http://www.senate.gov/~murkowski/

Sen. Patty Murry (WA)
http://www.senate.gov/~murray/

N   N

Sen. Don Nickles (OK)
http://www.senate.gov/~nickles/

Rep. Eleanor Holmes Norton (DC)
http://www.house.gov/norton/

Sec. Gale A. Norton
http://www.doi.gov/secretary/

O   O

Sandra Day O'Connor
http://www2.lucidcafe.com/lucidcafe/library/96mar/oconnor.html

Sec. Paul H. O'Neill
http://www.ustreas.gov/press/officers/oneill.htm

Rep. Solomon P. Ortiz (TX)
http://www.house.gov/ortiz/

If you find some dead links, please let us know at: http://www.celebritylocator.com/

P   P

Rep. Ron Packard (CA)
http://www.house.gov/packard/

Governor George E. Pataki (NY)
http://www.state.ny.us/governor/

Rep. Donald Payne (NJ)
http://www.house.gov/payne/

Rep. Nancy Pelosi (CA)
http://www.house.gov/pelosi/

Sec. Colin L. Powell
http://www.state.gov/secretary/

R   R

Rep. Charles B. Rangel (NY)
http://www.house.gov/rangel/

Justice William Rehnquist
http://www2.cybernex.net/~vanalst/william.html

Janet Reno
http://www.usdoj.gov/bios/jreno.html

Sen. Charles Robb (VA)
http://www.senate.gov/~robb/

Sen. John D. Rockefeller IV (WV)
http://www.senate.gov/~rockefeller/

Sec. Robert Rubin
http://www.ustreas.gov/

Sec. Donald Rumsfeld
http://www.defenselink.mil/pubs/almanac/osd.html

Gov. George H. Ryan (IL)
http://www.state.il.us/gov/

If you find some dead links, please let us know at: http://www.celebritylocator.com/

S _____ S

Justice Antonin Scalia
http://www2.cybernex.net/~vanalst/antonin.html

Sen. Charles Schumer (NY)
http://www.senate.gov/~schumer/

Sen. Richard Shelby (AL)
http://www.senate.gov/~shelby/

Sec. Rodney Slater
http://www.dot.gov/ost/

Sen. Olympia Snowe (ME)
http://www.senate.gov/~snowe/

Justice David Souter
http://www2.cybernex.net/~vanalst/david.html

Sen. Arlen Specter (PA)
http://www.senate.gov/~specter/

Sen. Ted Stevens (AK)
http://www.senate.gov/~stevens/

Gov. Jane Swift (MA)
http://www.state.ma.us/gov/gov.htm

T _____ T

Gov. Bob Taft (OH)
http://www.ohio.gov/gov/

Justice Clarence Thomas
http://www2.cybernex.net/~vanalst/clarence.html

Sen. Fred Thompson (TN)
http://www.senate.gov/~thompson/

Gov. Tommy Thompson (WI)
http://www.wisgov.state.wi.us/

If you find some dead links, please let us know at: http://www.celebritylocator.com/

Sen. Strom Thurmond (SC)
http://www.senate.gov/~thurmond/

V   V

Rep. Nydia Velazques (NY)
http://www.house.gov/velazquez/

Sec. Ann M. Veneman
http://www.usda.gov/agencies/gallery/veneman.htm

Gov. Jesse Ventura (MN)
http://www.governor.state.mn.us/

Sen. George Voinovich (OH)
http://www.senate.gov/~voinovich/

W   W

Sen. John Warner (VA)
http://www.senate.gov/~warner/

Rep. Maxine Water (CA)
http://www.house.gov/waters/

Rep. J.C. Watts (OK)
http://www.house.gov/watts/

Rep. Henry Waxman (CA)
http://www.house.gov/waxman/

Sen. Paul Wellstone (MN)
http://www.senate.gov/~wellstone/

Sec. Tango West
http://www.va.gov/welcome.htm

Prince William
http://www.gilmer.net/royalty/

If you find some dead links, please let us know at: http://www.celebritylocator.com/

Others

A   A

Dear Abby
http://www.uexpress.com/ups/abby/

Brandy Alexandre
http://www.kamikaze.org/

Angelie Almendare
http://www.angelie.com/

Avalon Anders
http://www.avalon-anders.com/

Carl Andrews, Jr.
http://www.carlandrews.com/

Anagha
http://www.anagha.com/

Dr. Maya Angelou
http://www.mayaangelou.com/

Piers Anthony
http://www.hipiers.com/

Roscoe "Fatty" Arbuckle
http://www.silent-movies.com/Arbucklemania/

Isaac Asimov
http://www.clark.net/pub/edseiler/WWW/asimov_home_page.html

B   B

Heywood Banks
http://www.heywoodbanks.com/

Clive Barker
http://www.clivebarker.com/

Tom Baxter
http://web.idirect.com/%7Etbhome/

If you find some dead links, please let us know at: http://www.celebritylocator.com/

Judy Blume
http://www.judyblume.com/

Jan Burke
http://www.janburke.com/

C _____ **C**

James Cameron
http://www.angelfire.com/id/amazingcameron/

Naomi Campbell
http://www.naomicampbell.com/

Carrot Top
http://www.carrottop.com/

Agatha Christie
http://www.agathachristie.net

Arthur C. Clark
http://www.lsi.usp.br/~rbianchi/clarke/

Michael Collins
http://www.michaelcollins.com/

David Copperfield
http://www.dcopperfield.com/

Douglas Coupland
http://www.coupland.com/

Cindy Crawford
http://www.cindy.com/

D _____ **D**

Diana, Princess of Whales
http://www.royal.gov.uk/start.htm

Salvador Dali
http://www.dali.com/

If you find some dead links, please let us know at: http://www.celebritylocator.com/

Tracy Dali
http://www.tracydali.com/

E _____ **E**

Amelia Earhart
http://www.ellensplace.net/ae_intro.html

Albert Einstein
http://www.westegg.com/einstein/

Emme
http://www.emmesupermodel.com/

Angie Everhart
http://www.geocities.com/Hollywood/Set/1345/

F _____ **F**

Fabio
http://www.northcoast.com/~shojo/Fabio/fabio.html

The Family Jewels
http://www.tfj.com/tfj/

Al Fike
http://www.alfike.com/

Ken Follett
http://www.ken-follett.com/

Glen Foster
http://www.glenfoster.com/

G _____ **G**

Gallagher
http://www.gallaghersmash.com/

Bill Gates
http://www.microsoft.com/BillGates/

If you find some dead links, please let us know at: http://www.celebritylocator.com/

Yasmeen Ghauri
http://www.td-sanchez.com/yasmeen/index.shtml

Martha Grimes
http://www.marthagrimes.com/

H   H

Prof. Stephen Hawkins
http://www.psyclops.com/hawking/

Eva Herzigova
http://www.iwcdesign.com/eva/

Alfred Hitchcock
http://www.primenet.com/~mwc/

Harry Houdini
http://www.uelectric.com/houdini/houdini.html

I   I

Kathy Ireland
http://www.kathyireland.com/

J   J

The Jerkyboys
http://www.thejerkyboys.com/

Pope John Paul II
http://www.vatican.va/
(another Pope John Paul II site)
http://www.zpub.com/un/pope/

Erica Jong
http://www.ericajong.com/

If you find some dead links, please let us know at: http://www.celebritylocator.com/

K   K

Dr. Jack Kevorkian
http://www.rights.org/~deathnet/KevorkianFile.html

Stephen King
http://www.stephenking.com/

Barbara Kingsolver
http://www.kingsolver.com/

L   L

Bob Larson
http://www.freespeech.org/boblarson/

Timothy Leary
http://leary.com/

Rush Limbaugh
http://www.rushlimbaugh.com/
(another Rush Limbaugh site)
http://www.rtis.com/nat/pol/rush/

David Lynch
http://www.davidlynch.com/

M   M

Elle MacPherson
http://www.microsaft.com/elle/

Cindy Margolis
http://www.cindymargolis.com/

Valeria Mazza
http://www.valeria.com.ar/

James A. Michener
http://www.jamesmichener.com/

If you find some dead links, please let us know at: http://www.celebritylocator.com/

Chris Moore
http://www.chrismoore.com/

Toni Morrison
http://www.luminarium.org/contemporary/tonimorrison/

Kate Moss
http://www.kate-site.com/

N _____ **N**

Cori Nadine
http://www.corinadine.com/

Nico
http://www.netpoint.be/abc/nico/

P _____ **P**

Bettie Page
http://www.grrl.com/betty.html

Vanessa Paradis
http://welcome.to/vanessa.paradis/

Penn & Teller
http://www.sincity.com/

Daniela Pestova
http://www.starpulse.com/Supermodels/Pestova,_Daniela/

Emo Philips
http://www.emophilips.com/

Edgar Allan Poe
http://www.comnet.ca/~forrest/

Maury Povich
http://gladstone.uoregon.edu/~wbeutler/maury.htm

Chef Paul Prudhomme
http://www.chefpaul.com/

If you find some dead links, please let us know at: http://www.celebritylocator.com/

R   R

Anne Rice
http://www.annerice.com/

Douglas Rushkoff
http://www.rushkoff.com/

S   S

Dr. Laura Schlessinger
http://www.drlaura.com/

Claudia Schiffer
http://www.claudiaschiffer.com/

Siegfried & Roy
http://www.siegfriedandroy-sarmoti.com/

Richard Simmons
http://www.richardsimmons.com/

Amber Smith
http://www.ambersmith.net/

Peter Sosna
http://pw1.netcom.com/~psosna/magic.html

Thomas Sowell
http://www.tsowell.com

Daniell Steel
http://www.daniellesteel.com/

Howard Stern
http://www.sternradio.com/

Gretchen Stockdale
http://www.gretchenstockdale.com/

Oliver Stone
http://www.geocities.com/Hollywood/2682/

If you find some dead links, please let us know at: http://www.celebritylocator.com/

T   T

Amy Tan
http://www.luminarium.org/contemporary/amytan/

Quentin Tarantino
http://www.geocities.com/SunsetStrip/Alley/7829/quentinsite.html

Scott Thompson
http://www.scottland.com/scott.htm

Christy Turlington
http://www.christy.org/

V   V

Frederique Van der Wal
http://www.supermodel.com/featured/frederique/

Dr. Jack Van Impe
http://www.jvim.com/

Vendela
http://www.vendela.net/

W   W

Alice Walker
http://www.luminarium.org/contemporary/alicew/

Andy Warhol
http://www.warhol.dk/

Dr. Bill Wattenburg
http://www.pushback.com/Wattenburg/

William Wegman
http://www.wegmanworld.com/

Tom Wolfe
http://www.tomwolfe.com/

If you find some dead links, please let us know at: http://www.celebritylocator.com/

E-mail Addresses

-A-

Kathryn Alison Acker
kathryn@newenglandtalent.org

Scott Adams
scottadams@aol.com

Daniel Adlerman
Bookkids@aol.com

Kim Adlerman
kimarts@aol.com

Aerosmith
vindaloo@hooked.net

Eddie Albert
eddie@eddiealbert.com

Agape
sabbi@limestone.kosone.com

Marilyn Agee
mjagee@kiwi.net

Alice in Chains
AICFC@speakeasy.org

Tim Allen
tim@morepower.com

Allman Brothers
rowlanda@allmanbrothersband.com

Angelie Almendare
mail@angelie.com

Amy Alpine
amyalpine@aol.com

Rosalyn Alsobrook
r.alsobrook@genie.geis.com

Amazing Randi
76702.3507@compuserve.com

Kevin J. Anderson
kevreb@aol.com

Pamela Anderson-Lee
pambonell@aol.com

Paul Anka
ANKAPA@aol.com

Jennifer Anniston
jeffr48196@aol.com

Ann-Margret
AMOSMAIL@aol.com

Piers Anthony
hi-piers@ix.netcom.com

Arianna
arianna@ariannausa.com

Jane Asher
info@jane-asher.co.uk

Kaitlyn Ashley
monty17@msn.com

Ed Asner
72726.357@compuserve.com

Asphalt Canyon
noodle@sirius.com

Audio Adrenaline
bobaa@aol.com

-B-

Baby Alive
xemu@xemu.com

If you find some incorrect addresses, please let us know at: http://www.cclebritylocator.com/

Celebrity Web Site & E-Mail Directory

Bad Boy Entertainment
bad.boy@bmge.com

Scott Bairstow
Scott@fansource.com

Oksana Baiul
fnemporium@aol.com

Melissa Baldwin
lissabee@cts.com

Tyra Banks
lucy56@aol.com

Bob Barker
price@www.cbs.com

John Perry Barlow
barlow@eff.org

Nevada Barr
NevadaBarr@compuserve.com

Sara Barrett
fanmail@sarabarrett.com

Paul Bearer
WWFBearer@aol.com

Pat Benatar
cowgirl@pacificnet.net

Richard Benjamin
richard@fansource.com

Darren Bennett
nflaussie@aol.com

Nigel Bennett
NBenn81369@aol.com

Sen. Joseph A. Biden
senator@biden.senate.gov

Craig Biggo
hof2ndbaseman@hotmail.com

Larry Bird
LarryBird3@aol.com

Scott Blackwell
NSoul@aol.com

Bill Blair
tmartin@bmi.net

Bone Thugs N Harmony
Leathafase@aol.com

Evan Bonifant
MrsBonifant@evanbonifant.com

J.R. Bookwalter
tempe@earthlink.net

Gillian Bonner
webmistress@blackdragon.com

Boston
bandmail@Boston.org

George Boyce
glenara@aol.com

David Boyd
dboyd@eworld.com

Sen. Barbara Boxer
Senator@Boxer.senate.gov

Bruce Boxleitner
bruce@fansource.com

Bozo The Clown
BOZO@tribune.com

Pat Brady
PBradyRose@aol.com

If you find some incorrect addresses, please let us know at: http://www.celebritylocator.com/

Sen. John Breaux
senator@breaux.senate.gov

David Brenner
hibrenner@aol.com

Tom Brokaw
nightly@nbc.com

Dr. Bill Bright
elvin@mdalink.com

Alan Brimm
bfa@slip.net

James L. Brooks
72700.2062@compuserve.com

Brooks & Dunn
BrooksDunn@brooks-dunn.com

Rep. George Brown
talk2geb@mail.house.gov

Jerry Brown
75300.3105@compuserve

Sen. Richard Bryan
senator@bryan.senate.gov.

Zachery Bryan
zachery@morepower.com

Pat Buchanan
76326.126@compuserve.com

Mike Burger
mikeb@homeandfamily.com

Delta Burke
Info@DeltaBurke.com

Jan Burke
jan@janburke.com

CH Burnett
chburn@execpc.com

Sen. Conrad Burns
conrad_burns@burns.senate.gov

Gov Jeb Bush
fl_governor@eog.state.fl.us

Robert Byrd
senator_byrd@byrd.senate.gov

-C-
Nicholas Cage
niccage@hotmail.com

Bruce Campbell
bcact@aol.com

Drew Carey
DrewsCShow@aol.com

Jim Carrey
jim@fansource.com

Gov. Paul Cellucci
GOffice@state.ma.us

Center of Attention
mbros@sils.umich.edu

Vinton Cerf
vcerf@CNRI.va.us

Sen. John Chafee
senator_chafee@chafee.senate.gov

Jackie Chan
jackie@jackiechan.com

Charo
fanclub@charo.com

If you find some incorrect addresses, please let us know at: http://www.celebritylocator.com/

Celebrity Web Site & E-Mail Directory

The Choir
choirline@aol.com

Tom Clancy
tomclancy@aol.com

Terry Ike Clanton
clanton1@ix.netcom.com

Blake Clark
Blakeman22@aol.com

Roger Clemens
roger.clemens@bluejays.ca

Hillary Rodham-Clinton
senator@clinton.senate.gov

Kristen Cloke
kristen@kristencloke.com

George Clooney
g_clooney@nbs.er.com

Coal Chamber
coalchamber@mysti.com

Claudia Christian
webmistress@claudiachristian.net

Kristi Coasts
wdz@ix.netcom.com

Sen. Thad Cochran
senator@cochran.senate.gov

Allan Cole
75130.2761@compuserve.com

Steve Coleman
mbase@epix.net

Jamie Owens Collins
dwc@earthlink

Judy Collins
rmprod@aol.com

Sean "Puffy" Combs
PuffyDad35@aol.com

Coolio
coolio@gangster.com

Tommy Coomes
coomesie@aol.com

Sen. Kent Conrad
HomePage@conrad.senate.gov

Continuim
danb@baronet.demon.co.uk

Rep. John Conyers
John.Conyers@mail.house.gov

Lydia Cornell
LYDIAC000@aol.com

Country Gamblers Band
lwarren@adsnet.com

Yvonne Craig
batgirl@yvonnecraig.com

The Cranberries
fnemporium@aol.com

Quentin Crisp
HRHQCrisp@aol.com

Jason Cropper
jchopllll@aol.com

Sheryl Crow
sherylcrow@thelot.com

Crowdies House
jraymond2@compuserve.com

If you find some incorrect addresses, please let us know at: http://www.celebritylocator.com/

Celebrity Web Site & E-Mail Directory

Tom Cruise
agoodactor@aol.com

Brett Cullen
brett@brettcullen.com

The Cure
thecure@thecure.com

Adam Curry
adam@metaverse.com

Billy Ray Cyrus
brcspirit@aol.com

-D-
Mark Dacascos
dacascos-mail@weblore.com

Dakoda Motor Co.
mbisonl@aol.com

Tracy Dali
tracydali@tracydali.com

Timothy Dalton
GSFE@aol.com

Rodney Dangerfield
rodney@rodney.com

Linda Dano
ldano@lindadano.com

Sen. Tom Daschle
tom_daschle@daschle.senate.gov

Dave Matthews Band
dmband@redlt.com

Greg Davis
duffers@halcyon.com

Bruce Davison
bruce@allmediapr.com

Dead Family
ari@deadfamily.com

Dead Man's Curve
deadman@jukebox.demon.co.uk

Calvert DeForest
:calvert@calvertdeforest.com

Johnny Depp
JohnnyDepp@rapidmail.com

Sen. Mike DeWine
webmaster@dewine.senate.gov

Diamond Rio
driofanclub@juno.com

Leonardo DiCaprio
dicaprio_@mailcity.com

Dick Dietrick
nitestnd@aol.com

Sen. Christopher Dobb
senator@dodd.senate.gov

Sen. Pete Domenici
Senator_Domenici@Domenici.Senate.Gov

The Doors
info@thedoors.com

Lesley-Anne Down
lesley-anne@fansource.com

David Duchovny
David.Duchovny@fox.com

If you find some incorrect addresses, please let us know at: http://www.celebritylocator.com/

Denice Duff
denice@deniceduff.com

Debbe Dunning
debbe@morepower.com

Alan Dysert
AlanDysert@songnet.com

-E-
Roger Ebert
73136.3232@compuserve.com

Clint Eastwood
rowdiyates@aol.com

Shari Eckert
shari@sharieckert.com

Barbara Eden
barbara@fansource.com

Emme
Emmemail@aol.com

Andrea Evans
webmistress@andreaevans.org

Greg Evans
geluann@aol.com

-F-
Kevin Fagan
kevinfagan@aol.com

Morgan Fairchild
morgan@fansource.com

Faze Productions
Faze_Productions@eriss.com

Sen. Dianne Feinstein
senator@feinstein.senate.gov

Giselle Fernande
gfernandez@nbc.com

Ferron
ferronfan@FerronWeb.com

Paul Fieg
heyhiboy@aol.com

Al Fike
alfike@usa.net

First Church of Chumbawamba
feedback@chumba.com

John Fischer
JWFisher@aol.com

Raymond Floyd
rayfloyd@rayfloyd.com

Focus
jmfocus@aol.com

Ross Forman
ROSSWCW@aol.com

Vivica Fox
vivica@vivicafox.com

Fournier Francine
FrancineECW@webtv.net

Robert Fulghum
70771.763@compuserve.com

-G-
Garbage
garbagezone@garbage.com

William "Bill" Gates
billg@microsoft.com

If you find some incorrect addresses, please let us know at: http://www.celebritylocator.com/

Celebrity Web Site & E-Mail Directory

Jennifer Gatti
jennifer@jennifergatti.com

Mac Gayden
gayden1@boone.net

Rep. Richard Gephardt
gephardt@mail.house.gov

Mel Gibson
mel_gibson@hotmail.com

Melissa Gilbert
melissa@fansource.com

Chuck Girard
chuck@chuck.org

Leigh-Davis Glass
leigh-davisglass@leigh-davisglass.com

Seth Godin
sgp@sgp.com

Goldberg
Annihil8or@wcwwrestling.com

Sen. Bob Graham (FL)
bob_graham@graham.senate.gov

Amy Grant
amy.grant@nashville.com

Jack Graue
oopinmoo@msn.com

Linda Gray
linda@fansource.com

The Greaseman
GreaseShow@aol.com

Martha Grimes
grimesinfo@plesser.com

The Gumbi Band
theband@thegumbiband.com

-H-
Senator Chuck Hagel
chuck_hagel@hagel.senate.gov

Merle Haggard
merle@merlehaggard.com

Deidre Hall
cjp@marlena.com

Hanson Brothers
hansonfans@hansonline.com

Senator Tom Harkin
tom_harkin@harkin.senate.gov

Senator Orrin Hatch
senator_hatch@Hatch.senate.gov

Dennis Hayden
dennis@dennishayden.com

Salma Hayek
salma@fansource.com

Isaac Hayes
fanmail@isaachayes.com

Brenda Henson
sisterspir@aol.com

Wanda Henson
sisterspir@aol.com

Faith Hill
faithfan@thebook.com

If you find some incorrect addresses, please let us know at: http://www.celebritylocator.com/

Earl Hindman
earl@morepower.com

Don Ho
dhoel@lava.net

Xaviera Hollander
Xaviera@xs4all.nl

Nancy Honeytree
jr@onehundred.com

Bob Hope
Bobhope@bobhope.com

Sir Anthony Hopkins
sirhopkins@aol.com

Larry Howard
LHBluesman@aol.com

Lisa Howard
earth@roddenberry.com

Brit Hume
72737.357@compuerserve.com

Sean Hurley
smhurley@micron.net

Olivia Hussey
frzflame24@earthlink.net

Rep. Asa Hutchinson
Asa.Hutchinson@mail.house.gov

Sen. Kay Bailey Hutchison
senator@hutchison.senate.gov

-I-
Initial Charge Band
xemu@xemu.com

Boman Irani
boman@bomanirani.com

Insane Clown Posse
JellyNuts@insaneclownposse.com

-J-
Jack Mack & The Heart Attack
jpbp@aol.com

Kate Jackson
kate@fansource.com

Jana Jae
janajae.com

Jamiroquai
webmaster@jamiroquai.co.uk

Mike Jansen
Skyward@cris.com

Helen Jayne
helenjayne@msn.com

Senator Jim Jeffords
vermont@jeffords.senate.gov

Grant R. Jeffrey
grantr.jeffrey@sympatico.ca

Jewel
Jeweljk@aol.com

Ann Jillian
MgrAJAM1@aol.com

Don Johnson
katejones1@aol.com

Jimmy Johnson (cartoonist)
arlnjan@aol.com

If you find some incorrect addresses, please let us know at: http://www.celebritylocator.com/

Senator Tim Johnson
tim@johnson.senate.gov

Erica Jong
jongleur@pipeline.com

Wynonna Judd
wifc@nashville.net

-K-
Karl Pabst & the Blue Ribbon
kdpbluribn@aol.com

Casey Kasem
Casey1110@aol.com

Ronan Keating
ronan@hg4.com

Garrison Keillor
gkeillor@madmax.mpr.org

Dr. D. James Kennedy
djk@cr-online.com

Senator Ted Kennedy
senator@kennedy.senate.gov

Senator John Kerry
john_kerry@kerry.senate.gov

Marianne Kesler
coolspirit@juno.com

Alan Keys
70744.1235@compuserve.com

Rabih EL-Khawli
rkawli@echo-on.net

Sally Kirkland
SallyKirkland@webtv.net

Michael E. Knight
CBMouser@aol.com

Wayne Knight
71054.2032@compuserve.com

KRUSH
davem@fia.net

Senator Jon Kyl
info@kyl.senate.gov

-L-
Cheryl Ladd
cheryll@attglobal.net

Ricki Lake
rickilake@aol.com

Senator Mary Landrieu
senator@landrieu.senate.gov

Jamie Lauren
jamie@jamielauren.com

Kelly LeBrock
kelly@fansource.com

Danni Leigh
info@dannileigh.com

David Letterman
lateshow@pipeline.com

Senator Carl Levin
senator@levin.senate.gov

G. Gordon Liddy
potent357@aol.com

Rush Limbaugh
70277.2502@compuserve.com

If you find some incorrect addresses, please let us know at: http://www.celebritylocator.com/

Celebrity Web Site & E-Mail Directory

Rick London
force@c-gate.net

Jennifer Lopez
jennifer@fansource.com

Sen. Trent Lott
senatorlott@lott.senate.gov

Courtney Love
lilacs00@aol.com

Mark Lowry
marklowry@marklowry.com

Lucias Tokas Band
marto8@seacoast.com

Dawn Lyn
dawnw111@catalinalink.com

-M-
Madonna
Madonna@wbr.com

Bill Maher
pi@cis.compuserve.com

Mary Maitlin
marymcbs@cais.com

Manic Street Preachers
manics@manics.co.uk

Dr. Geoffrey March
gmarch@stars.sfsu.edu

Cindy Margolis
cindcen@aol.com

Kitty Margolis
kittym@kittymargolis.com

Marky Mark
marky@kalifornia.com

Kellie Maroney
contact@kellimaroney.com

Pamela Sue Martin
pamsuemart@aol.com

Dana Mase
dana@danamase.com

MasterP
schmid@masterp.org

Chase Masterson
chase@chasemasterson.com

Dave Matthews Band
fanmail@dmband.com

Dawson McAllister
dmlive@christianradio.com

Sen. John McCain
John_McCain@McCain.senate.gov

Jenny McCarthy
jmccarthy@mailcity.com

Kimberly M'Carver
kimber@flash.net

Senator Mitch McConnell
senator@mcconnell.senate.gov

Maureen McCormick
mccormick@ttinet.com

Julie McCullough
JulieMcCul@aol.com

Bobby McFerrin
info@bobbymcferrin.com

If you find some incorrect addresses, please let us know at: http://www.celebritylocator.com/

Celebrity Web Site & E-Mail Directory

Roger McGuinn
rmcguinn@ix.netcom.com

Brian McKnight
brian@fansource.com

William McNamara
mcnamara@servtech.com

Jim Meddick
JimMeddick@aol.com

Leslie Meek
leslie@smartnet.net

Melon Patch
melonheads@aol.com

Men out Loud
menoutloud@earthlink.net

Metallica
metclub@aol.com

Alyssa Milano
angell@primenet.com

Mista Tru
Mista_tru@juno.com

Moby Grape
MobyGrape@Geocities.com

Katy Moffatt
kmwhq@mcleodusa.net

Eddie Money
EDDIEMNY@aol.com

T.S. Monk
tsmonk@jazzcorner.com

John Michael Montgomery
jmm@johnmichael.com

Demi Moore
Demim2aol.com

Glen Morgan
Gam5@aol.com

Alanis Morissette
fyiam@aol.com

Toni Morrison
morrison@princeton.edu

Bob Mortimer
bobmortimer@hotmail.com

Sen. Daniel P. Moynihan
Senator@dpm.senate.gov

Kate Mulgrew
kmulgrew@rocketmail.com

Sen. Frank Murkowski
email@murkowski.senate.gov

Sen. Patsy Murray
senator_murray@murray.senate.gov

-N-
Kathy Najimy
KathyNajimy@hotmail.com

Kevin Naylor
knaylor@digitalexp

David Nelson Band
dnb@nelsonband.com

Gunnar Nelson
GunNelson@aol.com

Matthew Nelson
MatNelson@aol.com

If you find some incorrect addresses, please let us know at: http://www.celebritylocator.com/

Willie Nelson
willie@willienelson.com

Wayne Newton
waynenewton@mailcity.com

Stevie Nick
stevie@fanmailink.com

Sen. Don Nickles
senator@nickles.senate.gov

Anna Nicole
live@annalive.com

Nichelle Nichols
nichelle@uhura.com

Brigitte Nielsaen
brigitte@fansource.com

Barbara Niven
barbara@barbaraniven.com

Mike Nesmith
nez@primenet.com

Kathleen Noone
kathleen@allmediapr.com

Ted Nugent
75162.2032@compuserve.com

Bill Nye
billnye@nyelabs.com

-O-
Oak Ridge Boys
jon@oakridgeboys.com

Oasis
oasis@oasisinet.com

Conan O'Brien
latenight@nbc.com

Miles O'Brien
70230.2064@compuserve.com

Renee O'Connor
RocMailer@aol.com

Rosie O'Donnell
(contact at website below)
http://rosieo.warnerbros.com/cmp/contact.htm

Edward James Olmos
lmh@kepplerassociates.com

Ashley Olsen
MKAFunClub@aol.com

Mary Kate Olsen
MKAFunClub@aol.com

Once Hush
oncehush@finetune.co

Yoko Ono
Yoko@yoko.com

Joan Osborne
joan-osborne@rockweb.com

Ozzy Osbourne
WORLDOFOZZ@aol.com

Rick Overton
72162.1701@compuserve.com

-P-
Sarah Jessie Parker
sis0386@aol.com

Julie Parrish
JParr18031@aol.com

If you find some incorrect addresses, please let us know at: http://www.celebritylocator.com/

Celebrity Web Site & E-Mail Directory

Gram Parsons
larryk@customeraccess.com

Gov. George Pataki
gov.pataki@chamber.state.ny.us

Ashley Peldon
ashley@allmediapr.com

Courtney Peldon
courtney@allmediapr.com

Lisa Pelikan
lisa@fansource.com

Jillette Penn
penn@delphi.com

Ross Perot
71511.460@compuserve.com

John Perry
barlow@eff.org

Pessimist Black Death Metal
pess666@ix.netcom.com

Bernadette Peters
WEBMASTER@BERNADETTEPETERS.NET

Mike Peters
grimmy@gate.net

Petra
petra@wordrecords.com

Phish
info@phish.net

Lincoln Pierce
drawnate@aol.com

Mandie Pinto
pntobmr@aol.com

Brad Pitt
rodrigocotasauce@hotmail.com

The Platters
info@theplatters.com

Jean-Luc ponty
jean-luc@ponty.com

Paula Poundstone
paula@mojones.com

Stefanie Powers
stefanie@fansource.com

Paula Prentiss
paula@fansource.com

Hillary Price
hprice@aol.com

Pat Priest
priest000@aol.com

Primus
bobcock@primussucks.com

Chef Paul Prudhomme
info@chefpaul.com

-R-
Lynn Redgrave
lynn@redgrave.com

Reel Big Fish
Reelbgfish@aol.com

Keanu Reeves
reeves23@aol.com

Ernie Reyes, Jr.
contact_erniejr@erniereyesjr.com

If you find some incorrect addresses, please let us know at: http://www.celebritylocator.com/

E-Mail Addresses

Celebrity Web Site & E-Mail Directory

Burt Reynolds
smokeymail@aol.com

Denise Richards
monacok@yahoo.com

Patricia Richardson
patricia@aol.com

Don Rickles
dj@hifrontier.com

Leann Rimes
larfans@leann.com

Geraldo Rivera
GeraldoCBS@aol.com

Sen. Charles S. Robb
senator@robb.senate.gov

David Robinson
Noelh@theadmiral.com

Sen. John Rockefeller
senator@rockefeller.senate.gov

Majel Roddenberry
stinfo@roddenberry.com

Dennis Rodman
worm@rodman.org

Al Roker
Mailbag@roker.com

Charlotte Ross
charlotte@charlotteross.com

Ann Rule
annier37@aol.com

Buddy Ryan
BuddyRyan@aol.com

Jeri Lynn Ryan
scimedjo@dhc.net

Shayna Ryan
shaynaryan@aol.com

-S-
Buffy Saint-Marie
bsm@aloha.net

Summer Sanders
SummerSanders@medalists.com

Adam Sandler
sandler@cris.com

Marie Sansone
RiaABC@aol.com

Devon Sawa
dsawa@pacificcoast.net

John Schneider
JRSFWPS@aol.com

Sen. Richard Shelby
senator@shelby.senate.gov

Kenny Shepherd
KWSband@aol.com

Grant Show
grant-show@fan.net

Silverchair
mail@chairpage.com

Tucker Smallwood
Tuck914@aol.com

Amber Smith
ambersite@webtv.net-

If you find some incorrect addresses, please let us know at: http://www.celebritylocator.com/

Celebrity Web Site & E-Mail Directory

Beau Smith
BeauSmith@aol.com

Ozzie Smith
ozzies@ozziesmith.com

Taran Noah Smith
taran@morepower.com

Wesley Snipes
herukush@aol.com

Tom Snyder
latelateshow@cbs.com

Kevin Sorbo
kenvin@fansource.com

Soundgarden
sgfc@speakeasy.org

Britney Spears
britney@peeps.com

Sen. Arlen Specter
Senator_Specter@Specter.senate

Robin Spielberg
spobs@access.digex.net

Stephen Spielberg
ssberg@amblin.com

Squirrel Nut Zippers
snz@mindspring.com

Tim Stack
nightstand@segi-mail.com

Lisa Stahl
LisaStahl1@aol.com

Scott Stantis
thebuckets@aol.com

Danielle Steele
awsomed@aol.com

Steely Dan
STEELYDAN@STEELYDAN.COM

Jim Steinman
steinman@1webplaza.com

Howard Stern
stern@urshan.com

Ray Stevens
rstevens@raystevens.com

Sen. Ted Stevens
senator_stevens@stevens.senate.gov

Crystal Storm
seestorm@aol.com

John Stossel
stossel@abc.com

George Strait
fanclub@georgestraitfans.com

Rider Strong
letters@riderstrong.com

Superdrag
SDRAG7@aol.com

Andy Summers
info@andysummers.com

Alison Sweeney
alison@alisonsweeney.com

-T-
Ty Tabor
76702.3455@compuserve.com

If you find some incorrect addresses, please let us know at: http://www.celebritylocator.com/

Celebrity Web Site & E-Mail Directory

Stacy Taylor
Stacytylr@aol.com

Tenison Twins
twins@tenisontwins.com

Keith Thibedeaux
earth.people@juno.com

Allyson Thomas
allysin@hotmail.com

Jonathan Taylor Thomas
jonathan@morepower.com

Larry Thomas
info@larrythomasthesoupnazi.com

Sen. Fred Thompson
senator_thompson@thompson.senate.gov

Tool
toolband@well.net

Hunter Tylo
CJNA67C@prodigy.com

Tricky
aboo@primenet.com

-U-
Under The Bridge
kdc@bbs.gaianet.net.

Robert Urich
robert@roberturich.com

-V-
VH1
VH1Postal@aol.com

Steve Vaile
gemstone@teleport.com

Dr. Jack Van Impe
jvimi@vim.com

Greg Vaughn
GREGV000@aol.com

Gov. Jesse Ventura
jesse.ventura@state.mn.us

Asia Vieira
Asia558543@aol.com

Vigilantes of Love
VOLMail@aol.com

Violent Femmes
dv@vfemmes.com

Vitamin F
vitamin@aol.com

Voice of Purity
ca_cameron@yumaeld.k12.az.us

Jenna Von oy
pedrew@aol.com

-W-
Lindsay Wagner
lindsay@fansource.com

Bob Wall
Walltime@aol.com

Joe Walsh
raycraft@post.avnet.co.uk

Matthew Ward
mward@e-tex.com

Dick Warlock
DickWarlock@hotmail.com

If you find some incorrect addresses, please let us know at: http://www.celebritylocator.com/

Celebrity Web Site & E-Mail Directory

Sen. John Warner
senator@warner.senate.gov

Muse Watson
musewatson@mindspring.com

Rep. J.C. Watts
rep.jcwatts@mail.house.gov

Andrew Lloyd Webber
rucny@reallyuseful.com

Bill Welch
Bill.Welch@pressroom.com

Adam West
AdamBatman@aol.com

Bob West
bobwest1@aol.com

Byran White
ByranOK@aol.com

White Heart
WhiteHeart@curb.com

Christine Todd Whitman
cwhitman@rutgers.edu

Van Williams
VanWilliam@aol.com

Oprah Winfrey
harpo@interaccess.com

Steve Winwood
fanmail@stevewinwood.com

Annie Wood
bzzzshow@aol.com

James Woods
jameswoods@aol.com

Louise Woodward
support@louise.force9.co.uk

Chely Wright
webmaster@chely.com

Noah Wyle
noahwer@aol.com

Victoria Wyndham
webmaster@victoriawyndham.com

-X
Xuxa
xuxa@ibm.net

Y
Trisha Yearwood
webmaster@totallytrisha.com

Marty York
Doveboy9@aol.com

Young Dubliners
dubs@youngdubs.com

-Z-
Laurie Z
ZLAURIE@aol.com

Larry Zerne
LarryZerne@aol.com

If you find some incorrect addresses, please let us know at: http://www.celebritylocator.com/

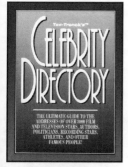

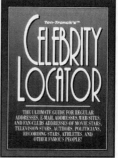